This book is a philosophical study of the content of mental representations of music. The central problem it addresses is as follows: how is it possible to describe a listener's cognition using music-theoretic concepts the listener does not possess? The author explains what it is for music cognition to be nonconceptual and how such mental representation contrasts with conceptual thought.

The author is both a philosopher and a musicologist and uniquely combines the perspectives of both disciplines. Exploring philosophical questions of mental representation in the relatively neglected, nonverbal domain of music, this study is a major contribution to the philosophical understanding of music perception and cognitive theory.

Music and Conceptualization

Music and Conceptualization

MARK DeBELLIS

Columbia University

CAMBRIDGE
UNIVERSITY PRESS

Published by the Press Syndicate of the University of Cambridge
The Pitt Building, Trumpington Street, Cambridge CB2 1RP
40 West 20th Street, New York, NY 10011-4211, USA
10 Stamford Road, Oakleigh, Melbourne 3166, Australia

First published 1995

Library of Congress Cataloging-in-Publication Data
DeBellis, Mark
Music and conceptualization / Mark DeBellis.
   p. cm.
Includes bibliographical references (p.) and index.
ISBN 0-521-40331-6
1. Music – Philosophy and aesthetics. I. Title.
ML3800.D3 1995
781'.11 – dc20   95-2405
             CIP
             MN

A catalog record for this book is available from the British Library.

ISBN 0-521-40331-6 Hardback

Transferred to digital printing 2004

Contents

Acknowledgments

I have been helped by many people in writing this book. I owe special thanks to Paul Benacerraf, who supervised the dissertation from which the book was developed and whose constant probing and criticism in response to my ideas at every stage served as a model and an inspiration. Both Gilbert Harman and Christopher Peacocke provided extensive comments on earlier drafts, suggested numerous avenues to pursue, and offered many points of clarification. I also profited from the remarks and advice of Akeel Bilgrami, James Dreier, Joseph Dubiel, Peter Kivy, Jonathan Kramer, Jerrold Levinson, Sidney Morgenbesser, Gideon Rosen, George Wilson, and participants in my seminar in philosophy of music cognition, Columbia University, in response to written and oral presentations of earlier versions of this material.

Sometimes it is hard to remember how one first became interested in a problem or topic. But I can trace my thinking about the themes of this book to conversations I had with my uncle, Michael de Bellis, some twenty years ago; for helping to point me down this road, I extend warmest thanks.

Finally, and most important, I want to thank my wife, Karla Johnsen, for her advice – always on target – on many aspects of this project and for her patience throughout.

Chapter 4 is reprinted with minor revisions from *Current Musicology* 55 (1993), pp. 56–87, by the kind permission of Columbia University. Chapter 5 originally appeared in Michael Krausz, ed., *The Interpretation of Music: Philosophical Essays* (Oxford: Oxford University Press, 1993). Chapter 6 is reprinted with minor revisions from Midwest Studies in Philosophy, Vol. 16: *Philosophy and the Arts*, Peter A. French, Theodore E. Uehling, Jr., and Howard K. Wettstein, eds., pp. 378–93, © 1991, by permission of the University of Notre Dame Press. Example 1.1 is reproduced from Ray Jackendoff, *Consciousness and the Computational Mind* (Cambridge, Mass.: MIT Press, 1987), p. 226, and Examples 2.6 and 3.2 from Fred Lerdahl and Ray Jackendoff, *A Generative Theory of Tonal Music* (Cambridge, Mass.: MIT Press, 1983), pp. 42 and 15, respectively, all with permission. Example 1.2 is reprinted from Heinrich Schenker, *Free Composition,* edited and translated by Ernst Oster, *Supplement: Musical Examples,* copyright © 1979, by permission of Schirmer Books/Simon & Schuster Macmillan.

This work was supported in part by an NEH Summer Stipend, fellowships from the Columbia University Council for Research in the Humanities, and a Chamberlain Fellowship from Columbia College, all of which I gratefully acknowledge.

Music and Conceptualization

1

Introduction: Hearing Ascriptions

1.1 What do we hear when we listen to music? This book is a philosophical study of the attempt to answer that question. It is about hearing ascriptions, statements of the form 'So-and-so hears such-and-such' originating in music theory and psychology, and the psychological states they attribute. It inquires into the meaning of such ascriptions and the nature of the states they ascribe.

On the view taken here, a hearing ascription attributes a state with a representational content, a state that represents a passage of music as being a certain way. The relevant questions are then what kind of content this is and how such psychological states compare and contrast with belief and thought.

I shall pursue and explicate the idea that musical hearing can be *nonconceptual*. In particular, I shall argue that the way an ordinary listener, untrained in music theory, hears music is nonconceptual in at least two main senses, which I call strong and weak respectively. Such hearing, I shall go on to argue, is to be contrasted with that of the trained music analyst, whose hearing is typically conceptual and theory-laden; musical training thus characteristically advances one's listening from a nonconceptual to a conceptual level. In the later chapters of the book I shall explore some of the cognitive and aesthetic issues that arise in connection with theory-laden musical perception.

Caveat: this is not a study of the representational content *of music*, but a study of the content of mental representations of music. Music may represent storms, Adam's fall from grace, or locomotives, but this semantic dimension of music is not our topic. It is rather the cognition of music, considered more or less syntactically, and the description of that cognition.

1.2   Example 1.1 represents an ascription of musical hearing as found in Fred Lerdahl and Ray Jackendoff's generative theory of tonal music (hereafter, GTTM).[1] The graph describes a certain way of hearing the passage, which, to a first approximation, involves hearing the B in measure 2 (all references are to the melody notes) as subordinate to the C# in m. 1, the first E in m. 1 as still more subordinate, and so on. The graph thus lays out a certain complex pattern of relationships and dependencies, specifying one way of hearing the passage.

This is an exciting prospect. It is exciting that the hearing of music should be susceptible to rich and detailed description in this way, that something so elusive and difficult to talk about can be captured in the net of a symbolic representation, a "mental map," as it were, of musical perception.

Though exciting, this prospect has its share of puzzles. What *is* it for a way of hearing a piece to correspond to such a representation? What property of hearing is captured by such a graph: at what level does it describe a mental representation of a piece? There is an assumption here that a perceptual state, or its content rather, may be specified via words or symbols – that the mental state and the symbolic representation used to attribute it are in some way equivalent

---

[1] Analysis given in Jackendoff (1987), p. 226, illustrating the theory presented in Lerdahl and Jackendoff (1983).

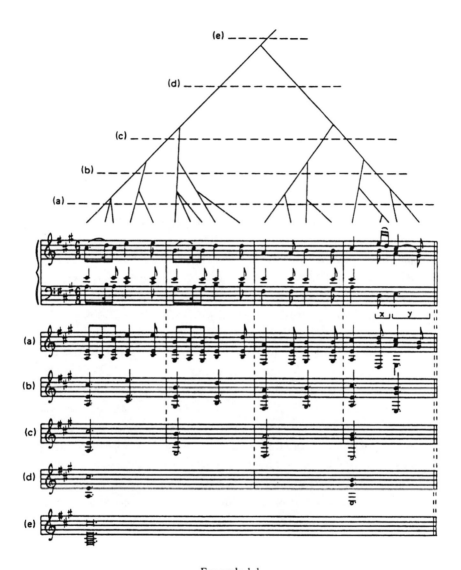

Example 1.1

in content.[2] But this demands explication. Is this sort of psychological attribution like (or an instance of) a belief report, and if so what kind of belief report? Is what we capture in such an attribution like what we capture when we attribute a thought to someone? How, in other words, is *hearing* music – in the way described by such a graph – related to *thinking* about it in that way? And how is this notion of hearing related to our ordinary notions of perception – the garden-variety sense in which we see colors and shapes, tables and chairs? What, in Wittgenstein's phrase, is the "place [of this notion of hearing] among the concepts of experience"?[3]

Puzzles arise, moreover, in trying to arrive at a coherent picture of our access to the facts expressed by these ascriptions that explains, at the same time, their interest to us. It is puzzling that we should find informative (and therefore strange and fascinating in a way) descriptions of what are after all *appearances* to us, descriptions that some of us can recognize as true. It seems impossible that we should be the authority for – have epistemic access to – the relevant facts and at the same time find them informative. Such are the semantic, psychological, and epistemological issues raised by the prospect of capturing musical hearing in words or symbols.

A (welcome) source of complication: GTTM is but one among many sources of hearing ascriptions. There are many accounts of hearing in music theory and psychology related to different levels of musical competence or understanding concomitant with different degrees of theoretical training.[4] There is a basic level of competence at which one recognizes familiar tunes, is able to detect obvious mistakes, and hears certain melodic configurations as complete and others as incomplete, though one does not know any music theory and is not able to explain why one hears those passages as one does.[5] It is this sort of competence that GTTM is primarily concerned to cap-

[2]Loar (1981), p. 31.
[3]Wittgenstein (1958), p. 193e.
[4]On levels of musical understanding, see Tanner (1985).
[5]For remarks on this basic sort of ability, see Dowling (1993a), p. 2.

ture. At a more sophisticated level of understanding, there are the self-descriptions of musical hearing by music analysts, whose competence includes an ability to describe their hearing in theoretical terms, an ability they owe in part to extensive aural training. There is no need to identify these different levels of hearing with one another. The questions posed earlier are multiplied, then, by the number of distinct kinds of musical competence there are: for any such concept of hearing we will want to know what that sort of hearing is, what its relation is to belief and thought, and so on. And we will want to know how such notions of hearing are related to, and contrast with, one another.[6] Most important, we will want to put those contrasts to use in order to characterize the differences between levels of musical competence or understanding.

One reason why it is plausible that different notions or levels of hearing are involved here is that the *same* music-theoretic vocabulary is often used in the description of more than one level of competence: it is one thing to hear intervals in the psychologist's sense, another in the ear-training teacher's. Therefore the distinction between such levels is not simply in the features perceived, but in the way they are perceived. The question, then, is how these different levels or notions of perception are to be distinguished from one another.

The problem is hinted at in a music appreciation text by Robert Winter:

You have been experiencing the elements of style – *rhythm* and *beat* and *meter*, for example – all your life. But now our goal is to translate those intuitive experiences into conscious ones.[7]

Winter is describing a certain program of aesthetic education, in which one moves from one level of musical understanding to another. These levels of understanding correspond to different levels of

---

[6]We should not be surprised if there are important differences among such notions. As Robert Cummins writes, "To suppose that [different cognitive theories] all make use of the same notion of representation seems naive" (1989, p. 12).

[7]Winter (1992), p. 15.

psychological ascription on which one may be said to hear, or experience, a certain rhythm or meter. The question is, what is the correct account of that distinction? Winter suggests one diagnosis: one level is "intuitive," another "conscious." But this is problematic: for what "experience" is not "conscious"?[8]

Many writers, like Winter, are inclined to appeal to the notion of consciousness in order to characterize the distinction between different levels of hearing.[9] This study takes a different tack: it is *conceptualization* that does the explanatory work. On this view, the distinction between conceptual and nonconceptual levels of representation is central to characterizing differences between levels of musical understanding; conceptualization is at the heart of growth in the appreciation and understanding of music. My purpose is to argue for these points and, more important, to explain what they mean, and to show what is necessary to establish them.

In recent years there has been much interest in articulating the ways in which perceptual experience and other kinds of mental representation may be regarded as nonconceptual.[10] One philosopher who has pointed to the importance of conceptualization for theories of musical understanding is Malcolm Budd, who writes:

To experience music with musical understanding a listener must perceive various kinds of musical processes, structures and relationships. But to perceive phrasing, cadences and harmonic progressions, for example, does not require the listener to conceptualise them in musical terms.[11]

---

[8]Of course, it would be unreasonable to expect a worked-out theory of these matters to appear in a music appreciation text; such a text should inspire the relevant growth, not give a theory of it. I quote Winter simply because the passage aptly points to the problem.

[9]E.g., Jackendoff (1987), p. 293; Levy (1983), pp. 101, 169–72; Meyer (1956), pp. 25, 50–2.

[10]See Crane (1992a) for a general discussion.

[11]Budd (1985), p. 247. The suggestion that musical understanding need not involve conceptualization can also be found in Meyer (1973), p. 16.

Budd's suggestion amounts to this: a correct psychological attribution of musical hearing can be made using music-theoretic concepts the listener does not possess. And this is one meaning that might be given to the claim that musical hearing (of a certain kind) is nonconceptual.

In the next chapter, I shall argue for a version of Budd's claim on which a concept is taken to be – or, rather, to be individuated by – a mode of presentation of a property. The claim will be established, then, by Fregean considerations of cognitive significance, whereby the statement that a passage has the relevant property has an information value distinct from that of the perceptual state thereby described. That perceptual state, in other words, is epistemically distinct from the belief expressed by the relevant music-theoretic sentence. This shows that these kinds of hearing and thought are conceptually distinct. In contrast, however, a trained listener's perceptual concepts are typically integrated with theories of music and analytic frameworks. The present analysis locates the contrast between such listeners, then, in terms of epistemic and informational relations rather than, say, the comparatively murky notion of consciousness.

But there are different degrees of nonconceptuality. For all that has been said, it is open that what is being attributed in these cases is, or essentially involves, some conceptual faculty or other, as long as those concepts are *different* from the music-theoretic ones employed in the attribution. Such psychological ascriptions may, in other words, attribute perceptual beliefs, involving perceptual concepts, as long as such concepts are distinct from the music-theoretic ones expressed by the relevant theoretical terms. This points to a stronger sense of "nonconceptual": musical hearing is nonconceptual in this sense if it is not a matter of the exercise of a conceptual faculty at all – if it is not perceptual belief. (I call this *strongly* nonconceptual, in contrast to the previous sense, which I call *weakly* nonconceptual.) I shall argue that an ordinary listener's musical hearing is strongly nonconceptual, too. The reason it is strongly nonconceptual is that

7

listeners typically cannot discriminate between events they represent in a certain way and events they do not represent in that way. But the possession of a perceptual concept goes hand in hand with a capacity for perceptual discrimination. The relevant sort of musical hearing is not the exercise, then, of a concept; it is not, *qua* type, a perceptual belief.

The ordinary listener's hearing differs from that of a trained listener, then, not only in being weakly nonconceptual but in being strongly nonconceptual. Higher levels of appreciation are laden with music-theoretic concepts. Such training thus characteristically makes conceptual what was, at most, formerly nonconceptual: it brings about conceptual representation of properties that the listener had heretofore represented, if at all, nonconceptually. (That is the view argued for here, although, as we shall see, something like the paradox of analysis arises for the case of the trained listener.)

The later chapters of the study address some of the issues surrounding theory-laden musical perception and its larger implications. One such issue is whether there is a tenable distinction between perception and cognition. Jerry Fodor has argued for such a distinction on the basis of modularity theory; Paul Churchland has claimed that musical training is a counterexample to Fodor's view. I shall argue that, given Fodor's own view of perception, basic aural tonal training is indeed such a counterexample.

In the last chapter I turn to the aesthetic issues surrounding theory-laden hearing, in particular, how such hearing contributes to understanding and enjoyment. I argue against a strong separation of the explanatory and appreciation-guiding functions of music theory. I claim rather that the explanatory power of theory-laden hearing is part and parcel of its aesthetic value. I then discuss puzzles that ensue.

1.3   Hearing ascriptions are descriptions of the musical mind in music theory and psychology. The ascriptions in which we are mainly interested are those of a structural or syntactic nature, as opposed to emotive descriptions such as 'He hears the music as sad (lively, majestic, etc.)'. Let us survey some examples and the contexts in which they occur.

One important source of hearing ascriptions is music analysis, which is part of the discipline of music theory. It entails the description of a musical work, detailing its structure and the relationships among its parts. There are many approaches to, and varieties of, music analysis, such as Schenkerian analysis, Forte's set theory, the semiotic approaches of Ruwet and Nattiez, and the systems of such theorists as Riemann, Réti, Keller, and LaRue; music analysts often draw upon such systems as well as more ad hoc approaches.[12] At the same time, there is much common ground: in the analysis of tonal music, for example, there is a shared framework that includes what might be called "traditional tonal theory," embracing such concepts as tonic, dominant, scale degrees, key areas, modulations, and the rhythmic and metrical features implied by conventional musical notation.

Probably the most influential and dominant paradigm in the analysis of tonal music in the United States is Schenkerian analysis, on which a tonal work is conceived of as an elaboration, or "prolongation," of simpler passages, iterated at several hierarchical levels.[13] This conception can be expressed in a graph via a specialized notation adapted from conventional music notation (Example 1.2).[14] In this notation, stems and durational symbols indicate structural importance.

Inseparable from music analysis are statements about hearing.

---

[12]The analytic systems listed here are surveyed in Bent (1987). Less comprehensive in scope, but a good pedagogical introduction to analytic practice, is Cook (1987a).

[13]Schenker (1979 [1935]), p. 5. In strict Schenkerian terminology, 'prolongation' designates a particular kind of elaboration rather than elaboration in general, but as Neumeyer and Tepping note, the term has taken on a wider sense than Schenker's original usage (1992, p. 3).

[14]From Schenker (1979 [1935]), vol. 2, ex. 7(a).

9

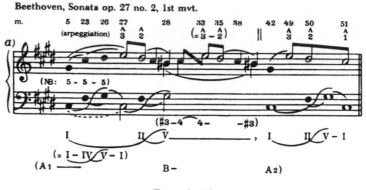

Example 1.2

"This [graph] . . . shows how I hear it."[15] "Harmonically, one can hear m. 3 as revolving around F, and m. 4 around G. In that case, the entire progression of mm. 1–5 can be heard as an expansion of the I–IV–V–I of the opening measure."[16] "It is . . . possible to hear the establishment of the D-flat triad in m. 49 as the arrival of tonic harmony."[17] "This rhythmic arrival is heard also as the beginning of a new hypermeasure."[18] "In order to hear and understand the significance of chords as passing chords and to enable the ear to penetrate to the structural goal of a motion, a sense for musical direction has to be developed."[19] "Compare and contrast the ways of hearing [a passage from a Mozart string quintet] represented in the two analyses [that follow]."[20]

Statements about hearing employing music-analytic vocabulary

[15]Cone (1968), p. 41.

[16]Ibid., p. 35.

[17]Krebs (1991), p. 49.

[18]Kramer (1988), p. 91. In much music analysis, the reference to hearing is implicit, but I do not claim that all music analysis is to be read in this way. See Chapter 6 for further discussion.

[19]Salzer (1962), vol. 1, p. 102.

[20]M.A. theory examination question, Columbia University. It is not uncommon for analysts to hypostatize "hearings," designated by analyses. See Krebs (1991), p. 51, and Kramer (1988), p. 130.

may also occur in related – for example, pedagogical – contexts: an ear-training teacher may say, in reporting the level achieved by students in an introductory course, something like 'They can hear tonics and dominants, but that's about it; they have a lot of trouble hearing intervals'.

Music analysts typically have extensive training in music theory, such as the systems mentioned earlier. Such training characteristically has a perceptual component: the basic aural training connected with tonal theory entails taking down melodies for dictation, singing melodies at sight, and so on.

A second, and I shall argue rather different, source of hearing ascriptions is cognitive psychology, a primary aim of which is to explain listeners' behaviors and abilities, such as melody recognition, error detection, and judgments of when a tonal melody is complete or incomplete.[21] In order to explain such abilities, cognitive psychologists hypothesize certain kinds of mental representations; and the attribution of such representations constitutes a second broad class of what I call hearing ascriptions. Various parameters have been taken to be represented on such theories – pitch, interval, and chroma, for example.[22]

It is important to note that the subjects described here form a much wider class than the musical analysts just discussed. They are what I call ordinary listeners: subjects who have a certain basic musical competence, but who know no music theory and have not received the aural training concomitant with music theory. (Precisely what level of basic competence this turns out to be will depend on the particular psychological theory at issue.)

One model of musical representation, to which we will make prominent reference in this study, is the relative chroma model. Rel-

---

[21]For general discussions of the aims and purposes of cognitive psychology of music, see Dowling (1993a) and Dowling and Harwood (1986).

[22]A useful overview of candidates for representation is given in Bharucha (1991), pp. 89–93. Other surveys and discussions of mental representation in music psychology can be found in Deutsch (1982) and Dowling (1982a).

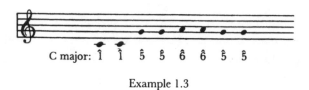

C major: $\hat{1}$ $\hat{1}$ $\hat{5}$ $\hat{5}$ $\hat{6}$ $\hat{6}$ $\hat{5}$. $\hat{5}$

Example 1.3

ative chroma can be defined in the following way. Pitches have the same absolute chroma if they have the same letter name; thus, all pitches labeled C-sharp, in any register, have the same absolute chroma. Chroma distance is distance between absolute chromas. And relative chroma is chroma distance relative to some reference point.[23] As it turns out, psychologists' notion of relative chroma is more or less equivalent to the music-theoretic notion of *scalestep*, or scale degree, which implies distance from a tonic, but abstracts from register.[24] (C is the first degree, $\hat{1}$, or tonic of C major; D the second degree, $\hat{2}$, or supertonic; G the fifth degree, $\hat{5}$, or dominant.)[25]

On the relative chroma model, a melody is mentally represented as a sequence of relative chromas. This is one model that has been proposed to explain the recognition of familiar melodies (Example 1.3).[26]

I would like now to discuss GTTM, a sample of which we en-

[23]This definition draws on Bharucha (1991), pp. 92–3.

[24]Dowling and Harwood (1986), p. 128. Actually, the notions of scalestep and relative chroma are not precisely equivalent, but are close enough for our purposes. One difference is that scalestep is regarded not as a continuum, but as a set of discrete locations, unlike chroma (Bharucha [1991], p. 93). Another difference is that scale degree is defined with respect not only to a tonic, but to a scale degree type such as major and minor. This generates a kind of equivalence between pitches of the same scale degree in different scale types – we can think of $\hat{3}$ in major as an "altered form" of $\hat{3}$ in minor, for example – not captured in any natural or straightforward way by chroma. I suppress these complications.

[25]From time to time, I shall draw on this equivalence for notational purposes, using scalestep notation – $\hat{1}$, $\hat{2}$, etc. – to designate chromas. The main philosophical points will not depend on this, however; other notations for chroma might be substituted.

[26]Dowling and Harwood (1986), pp. 128, 142, endorse a version of this model, as

12

countered earlier, more fully. Lerdahl and Jackendoff characterize GTTM as "music theory as psychology," modeling the theory after generative linguistics.[27] The principal aim of GTTM is to provide "a formal description of the musical intuitions of a listener who is experienced in a musical idiom."[28] Lerdahl and Jackendoff's notion of an experienced listener is that of one who is acculturated in a certain musical idiom but does not necessarily have musical training.[29] (This includes, but is not restricted to, what I have been calling an ordinary listener.)

GTTM posits five levels of musical organization: the musical surface, the grouping level, the metrical level, the time-span reduction level, and the prolongational reduction level.[30] Each level except the musical surface is hierarchical in nature. The musical surface consists of individual notes and chords, with specific pitches and durations.[31] On the grouping level, passages are segmented into motives, phrases, themes, sections, and so on.[32] The metrical level involves organization into strong and weak beats, measures, and larger

do Bharucha (1991), pp. 92–3, Idson and Massaro (1978), and Kallman and Massaro (1979). The main competitor of the relative chroma model is the successive interval model, which hypothesizes the representation of intervals between successive pitches rather than intervals with respect to some more or less constant reference point. What makes it plausible that intervals of one sort or another have to be postulated is that we can recognize a familiar melody under transposition when the absolute pitch locations are not preserved. This was one of the classic problems stated as a motivation for Gestalt psychology by von Ehrenfels (1937), p. 521. For empirical considerations in favor of the relative chroma model over the successive interval model, see Bharucha (1991), pp. 91–2; Davies (1978), p. 146; Davies and Jennings (1977), p. 539; and Dowling (1982b), p. 426.

[27]Lerdahl and Jackendoff (1983), p. 5.

[28]Ibid., p. 1.

[29]Ibid., p. 3.

[30]Ibid., pp. 8–10; see also Jackendoff (1987), pp. 218–33.

[31]Jackendoff (1987), p. 218.

[32]Lerdahl and Jackendoff (1983), p. 12.

units.[33] Each of the reductional levels, time-span and prolongation-al, treats musical passages as "ornamentations or elaborations" of simpler passages.[34] Of these, prolongational reduction, which involves tension and relaxation, is the more important; time-span reduction, an example of which was given earlier, may be thought of as a kind of stepping stone to prolongational reduction.[35]

GTTM is a theory of mental representation. It is intentionalistic through and through, referring to intuitions, knowledge, recognition, comprehension, and the attribution of organization.[36] A graph of GTTM is to be understood as occurring – perhaps implicitly – in the context of a psychological attribution such as 'An experienced listener hears this passage as _____ ' (where the blank is filled in with the graph).[37]

I wish to make two points about the aspects of GTTM that are particularly relevant for us. The first is that we are interested mainly in GTTM's structural descriptions of particular passages of music rather than the rule systems governing such descriptions that it seeks to infer. Arriving at such rule systems is, to be sure, a major goal, if not the central motivation, of GTTM. But in order to accomplish this, the theory must have data to work with, and such data include representations of particular passages. It is the status of the latter that will be our primary focus.[38]

[33]Ibid., pp. 19–21.

[34]Jackendoff (1987), p. 224.

[35]Lerdahl and Jackendoff (1983), p. 179. This characterization of time-span reduction as a preliminary stage is suggested in (1983), p. 121, and has recently been stated more explicitly by Lerdahl (1993).

[36]Lerdahl and Jackendoff (1983), pp. 3, 6. Jackendoff uses the term 'mental representation' explicitly in (1987), p. 218.

[37]There is some room for variation in the exact form we might think of such statements as taking. I shall return to this point shortly.

[38]Thus, we factor out of the discussion the interesting but independent question of whether GTTM's rule systems – analogous to grammars in natural language – are themselves mentally represented or objects of knowledge. One may take a different stance toward the status of grammars versus particular sentences, as Stich (1971,

The second point is that GTTM seems to be something of a hybrid of the music-analytic and cognitive-psychological approaches considered earlier. GTTM, like many theories in cognitive psychology, is intended to be true of listeners untrained in music theory. But the data for the theory – data specifying which structural descriptions are psychologically correct – have a prominent source in the "intuitions" of listeners who can read and understand such descriptions, most notably the authors of GTTM themselves (one of whom, Lerdahl, is a composer and music theorist). Thus, in GTTM we have kind of a combination of the music-theoretic and cognitive-psychological perspectives; we shall try to draw out some of the implications of this.

1.4   The foregoing constitute, then, some central sources and examples of hearing ascriptions. Now for some matters of notation and terminology. Though, as to their surface form, hearing ascriptions exhibit a certain amount of variation – a music analyst may say, 'I hear a dominant' or 'That [pointing to an analysis] is the way I hear the piece', or simply produce an analysis, leaving the talk of hearing implicit – it is convenient to abstract away from this surface variation and settle upon a canonical form, or schema, which we shall take to represent hearing ascriptions generally (or at any rate those in which we are interested). This is the schema:

(1a) [Listener] hears [sound-event] as a [music-theoretic kind],

or, using schematic letters,

(1b) S hears x as an F,

where 'S' is a placeholder for an expression that designates a listener, 'x' a placeholder for a sound-event, 'F' a placeholder for a music-

pp. 480–1) has pointed out. I am indebted to Christopher Peacocke for alerting me to this distinction.

theoretic or cognitive-psychological predicate and where 'hears' stands for itself as well as a range of verbs such as 'mentally represents' and 'perceives'.[39] Instances of this schema include

(2) I hear that pitch as a dominant

and

(3) She mentally represents the passage as grouped into two four-bar phrases.

One advantage of this formulation is that it avoids the distraction of an unintended reading of expressions such as 'I hear a dominant'. That expression has the reading 'There is something such that it is a dominant and I hear it', which – although it is certainly something one could conceivably want to say – is virtually never what a music theorist means by 'I hear a dominant'.[40] We lose nothing essential for our purposes if we recast it as, or consider instead, 'I hear that as a dominant'; hence, I shall concentrate on statements of the latter form.

Hearing ascriptions constitute our point of departure. Our approach follows analytic philosophy's time-honored practice of starting with a segment of discourse and analyzing it, or asking what it means. The terminology I have adopted has, of course, been meant to suggest an analogy with belief ascriptions: and whether hearing ascriptions *are* belief ascriptions, not just analogous to them, is a question we shall take up. At the same time, our project is not exclusively semantic, since we are concerned also with the nature of the

---

[39]By a sound-event I mean a token sounded on a particular occasion, which may be a note or chord, a passage, or an entire work. This notion of a sound-event is derived from Walton (1988), p. 241. For simplicity I ignore statements resulting from quantification, such as statements about all listeners of a certain kind and all tonal passages.

[40]On that reading, I would hear a dominant if, for example, the sound of a piano

psychological states hearing ascriptions ascribe, which is not a purely linguistic issue. As I have already indicated, I do not think that all hearing ascriptions are on a par in semantic and psychological respects; my point is to show how such differences are associated with different kinds or levels of musical competence.

But there is an issue here about how the domain of inquiry is to be taxonomized. Hearing ascriptions cannot be individuated solely on the basis of spelling, since we are going to want to say that something of the form '*S* hears *x* as $\hat{3}$' has a different meaning in the context of ear training versus the chroma theory, for example. I shall assume that we have a sufficiently clear notion of hearing-ascription *types* such that all tokens of the same type will receive the same analysis; such types will serve as our primary objects of inquiry. It seems at least approximately true that such types are relative to, and individuated by, theories.[41] (In what follows, by a hearing ascription I shall mean a type, unless otherwise noted.)

I shall assume that, for any type of hearing ascription, there is a type of psychological state that it names, a state one is in just in case one satisfies the ascription; I shall call such a state (musical) *hearing*.[42] (There may be as many different kinds of hearing as types of hearing ascription.)

To sum up things so far, our project will take the form of an analysis of hearing ascriptions and an inquiry into the nature of mu-

---

were barely audible through the soundproofed wall of the next room and I heard a kind of muffled thump, where that sound was in fact a dominant pitch or chord. But ordinarily, 'I hear a dominant' is meant to be a stronger claim than this.

[41]To be sure, there is some vagueness in this, since it is not always clear which theory a musical analyst implicitly invokes on a given utterance of 'hears'; moreover, it seems doubtful that an analyst always invokes something well defined and systematic enough to be called a theory. I suppress these complications.

[42]More properly, the state is *named* by the expression schema 'hearing . . . as an *F*' and is *ascribed* by the corresponding hearing ascription, but I will not trade on this qualification.

sical hearing. In what follows, I take the stance that hearing is representational and try to illuminate how it is representational: to say what sort of mental representation hearing is and what sort of content it has. But I must explain and motivate this stance, and so to this we now turn.

2

Musical Hearing as
Weakly Nonconceptual

2.1 It is a central assumption of this study that musical hearing is representational and that hearing ascriptions are representational ascriptions. But what does this mean?

To say that musical hearing is representational means, first and foremost, that it has a satisfaction condition. In hearing a passage, one represents it as being a certain way, where it is meaningful to ask whether the passage *is* that way – that is, whether one's mental representation is true of, is satisfied by, the passage.[1] More generally, being a representation entails having a content, something the representation is about, means, or expresses. Satisfaction conditions constitute one level of content, but there are others, as I shall explain.

To say that a hearing ascription is a representational ascription means that it characterizes a hearing state at a representational level, that is, in terms of its content. I assume, moreover, that the use of

[1]"The word 'true' indicates the aim of logic, as does 'beautiful' that of aesthetics or 'good' that of ethics" (Frege [1956], p. 289).

19

music-theoretic terms for psychological attribution is semantically and conceptually posterior to their use to describe *music:* the semantic properties of 'hears . . . as a dominant' depend on those of 'is a dominant', and our understanding of what it is for someone to hear a pitch as a dominant depends on a prior understanding of what it is for a pitch to *be* a dominant.[2]

Why should we view musical hearing, and its ascription, as representational in this way? Is it the only possible conception?

One alternative has been clearly stated by Christopher Peacocke.[3] In a discussion of sense experience, Peacocke draws a distinction between two kinds of properties of experience: representational properties, which are properties an experience has in virtue of representing the world as being a certain way, and sensational properties, which are "properties an experience has in virtue of some aspect – other than its representational content – of what it is like to have that experience."[4] Alleged sensational properties are size in the visual field and the feeling of depth that is characteristic of binocular vision.[5] Peacocke holds, moreover, that certain experiences lack representational properties entirely, such as visual experiences one has when one closes one's eyes and faces the sun.[6]

I will not attempt to evaluate here the overall tenability of the representational–sensational distinction. What is relevant for us is, rather, Peacocke's assimilation of grouping phenomena, such as those investigated in Gestalt psychology, to sensational qualities.[7] On Peacocke's view, the difference between seeing an array of dots as or-

---

[2]I take it, moreover, that for any *F* the state of hearing a sound-event as an *F* has the same satisfaction conditions as the expression '*x* is *F*' (perhaps among other levels of content).

[3]Peacocke (1983). His views have since changed; see, e.g., Peacocke (1992b), p. 82. But for purposes of exposition it is helpful to go back to Peacocke (1983). I discussed these issues earlier in DeBellis (1988) and (1991).

[4]Peacocke (1983), p. 5.

[5]Ibid., pp. 12–13.

[6]Peacocke (personal communication, 1990).

[7]Again, this is on the Peacocke (1983) account.

ganized into rows and as organized into columns is a difference in sensational properties. And, he suggests, so is the difference between hearing a succession of drumbeats as organized into groups of two and hearing such a succession as organized into three, or between hearing two pitches as an augmented fourth and as a diminished fifth.[8]

Assimilating certain aspects of musical hearing to sensational properties of experience is one alternative, then, to what I have been calling a representational conception of musical hearing. (And likewise for its ascription: to say that someone hears a succession of beats in twos rather than threes or an interval as an augmented fourth rather than a diminished fifth is, on this view, to say something about the sensational, rather than representational, properties of that listener's experience.) Another proponent of what I regard as a nonrepresentational conception, if I read him right, is Jackendoff, who embraces the "Mentalist Postulate" that "meaning . . . is an information structure that is mentally encoded by human beings."[9] Jackendoff understands this to mean that semantics should not be concerned primarily with truth conditions; by his lights, semantics rightly conceived "locates meanings in the computational mind."[10] To be sure, Jackendoff calls the relevant mental structures "representations," but I say that without truth conditions they would be representations in name only: they would not represent musical passages *as being* any way or other, and hence would not be so much representations as responses.

A nonrepresentational view of musical hearing does not have the same implications for the relation between 'hears . . . as a dominant' and 'is a dominant' as a representational view. (Here 'dominant' stands in for any music-theoretic predicate.) If hearing is not representational, there is no need to suppose that 'is a dominant' is semantically and conceptually prior to 'hears . . . as a dominant'. As-

---

[8]Ibid., p. 25.

[9]Jackendoff (1987), p. 122.

[10]Ibid., p. 129. Jackendoff takes a similar view in (1992), p. 165.

suming that 'is a dominant' has a use at all, there are two possibilities: either 'hears . . . as a dominant' is prior to 'is a dominant' – so that 'is a dominant' might be defined as a disposition to be heard as a dominant, in analogy with dispositional accounts of secondary qualities – or neither has priority over the other.[11]

The issue is this: are musical organization and other music-theoretic properties to be understood, in the first instance, as features of mental states or as features *of music* (which said mental states represent the music as having)? Here I opt for the latter conception. Let me briefly state why.

The first reason is that there seems to be no lack of plausible candidates for what the ways *are* that the relevant states represent the music as being. Consider grouping, for example. To begin with a visual example, suppose you see the figure shown in Example 2.1 as composed of three parts, A, B, and C (Example 2.2). The question is, for what value of X are you seeing the figure *as being X*? Answer: it is for the figure to be composed of the three parts A, B, and C (joined left to right) – that is, to be a certain aggregate or mereological sum of those parts. (The figure is also a mereological sum of other parts in countless ways, to be sure – for example, D and E [Example 2.3]. But that in no way detracts from its being a sum of A, B, and C.)

The perception of musical organization can be understood along similar lines. Take meter, for example. Hearing a sequence of notes in 6/8 (Example 2.4) might be analyzed as representing the duration of a bar as the sum of two constituent durations A and B (Example 2.5), and each of A and B as the sum of three constituent durations, and so on, at lower or higher hierarchical levels. Again, what the account takes to be represented here is a way the passage *is*. (And it does not count against this analysis that the interval of time is a sum of durations in many other ways as well.)

[11]As Peacocke (1983), pp. 28–30, points out, though he takes a view of secondary qualities on which 'red' is a semantic constituent of 'looks red'. For discussion, see Smith (1986).

Example 2.1

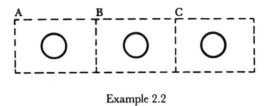

Example 2.2

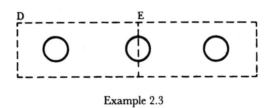

Example 2.3

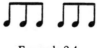

Example 2.4

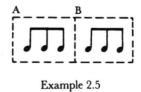

Example 2.5

Hence, one plausible candidate for what we hear a musical passage *as being,* when we hear meter, is the passage's being a certain mereological sum of durations; and this is a representational conception, since it takes our understanding of what it is to *be* such a sum to be prior to our understanding of what it is to *hear* the passage as such a sum. And, in general, there is no lack of plausible candidates for such contents.

A second reason for taking the representational conception has to do with the individuation and identity of the mental states we call hearing. Consider Jackendoff's "conceptualist semantics," which supposedly need not mention truth conditions. What, then, is the account that tells us what makes a given state inside one's head a token of this, rather than that, GTTM representation? What, in short, determines type-identity of GTTM's representations? Jackendoff does not tell us, and I strongly suspect that this question cannot be answered in any satisfying way that does not at the same time bring in truth conditions, thus supporting a representational conception.

A third reason why I take a representational view of musical hearing comes from the fact that I want to ask about the relations between hearing and thought. Thinking about a passage as having this or that music-theoretic property is surely representational, and the most straightforward approach is to compare like with like. I see no reason to amplify differences in logical form between 'hears x as a dominant' and 'thinks of x as a dominant' unless it is necessary. Thus, on this initial survey I follow considerations of simplicity; there is always the opportunity for more complicated approaches.[12]

---

[12]Two difficulties arise on a representational conception, which I shall note here but not attempt to address. First, not *every* aspect of a music-theoretic graph has to be understood as part of a content attribution: some features, such as designations of specific absolute pitch locations, can be thought of instead as fixing the referent, that is, specifying the sound-events heard. Second, it is often left unstated how a graph of an entire piece (or extended passage) is to be decomposed into individual attributions. No one hears a piece all at once, so presumably an analysis of a whole piece is to be understood as the conjunction of psychological attributions involving parts of

2.2 I take the view, then, that a hearing ascription ascribes a representational state to a listener and characterizes that state at a representational level – in terms of its content. A graph of GTTM is thus, as we have said, a kind of mental map. But it is not a map of a mental representation – of its intrinsic features involving neurons and synapses – so much as a map that specifies the mental representation's content, what that representation represents.[13] It is one representation used to characterize the representational power of another, something like a synonym or translation. Of course, psychological attributions are more commonly made with words than with tree diagrams or Schenkerian graphs, but that is a difference of language, not of logic.[14]

If (a given kind of) hearing is a representational state, what sort of mental representation is it? Is it a kind of thought, or, if not, how are (that kind of) hearing and thought related? What sort of content does it have? How are the contents involved in hearing a chord as a dominant, and thinking of it as a dominant, related? Are different kinds of hearing to be distinguished in that their contents are related differently to thought contents?

It is clear that at this point we need some moorings: an initially plausible starting point, or "null hypothesis," such that the burden of proof is on one who would refute it. Now it seems plausible to say that hearing ascriptions are about musical perception, and it is a

the piece. But it is often left unspecified where one attribution leaves off and another begins. These complications do not constitute serious problems for the representational conception per se, but show that care must be taken in formulating the relevant psychological attributions precisely.

[13]In Gilbert Harman's terminology, it specifies intrinsic features of the intentional object as contrasted with intrinsic properties of a psychological state. See Harman (1990), p. 41, and (1987), pp. 72–3.

[14]Goodman (1976) and Goodman and Elgin (1988) explore (from a different perspective than ours) the possibilities of using nonlinguistic symbols to attribute content.

more or less received and venerable view in the philosophy of perception that perception is a matter of acquiring *beliefs*.[15] It is thus at least plausible to suppose that hearing ascriptions ascribe beliefs acquired in musical perception. And, by Occam's razor, we should not multiply types of cognitive states beyond necessity: we should count perceptual states as beliefs unless we are forced to say otherwise. I shall take as our null hypothesis, then, that musical hearing is perceptual belief and hearing ascriptions are ascriptions of perceptual belief. I shall call this the *belief thesis*. (The thesis can be understood either as having separate instances for each kind of musical hearing or as the universally quantified claim that all kinds of musical hearing are perceptual belief, and so on; I shall rely on context to disambiguate these.) Hearing ascription is, on this hypothesis, not just *analogous* to belief ascription; it *is* one kind of belief ascription. In what follows, the belief thesis will constitute a point of reference: we will want to see whether it can be maintained, what further moves (if any) are required to maintain it, and what considerations count for or against it.

2.3 I shall argue now that there is a kind of musical hearing that is nonconceptual in a sense I call *weakly* nonconceptual. To see what this means, let us recall Budd's claim:

---

[15]The classic statement of this so-called epistemic view of perception has been given by Armstrong: see (1968), p. 208, and (1961). For further references see Pitson (1990), p. 74, n. 1. The essence of the view, disregarding qualifications and complications, is that perception is "nothing but" the acquiring of beliefs about the environment (Armstrong [1968], p. 242). Actually, all that is required for our purposes is a rather weaker premise: perception is a process that characteristically brings about such beliefs, whether or not that is all it consists in. Philosophers have disagreed over whether the acquisition of perceptual belief is "direct" or mediated by a relation to private mental objects (which is one meaning of "sense data"; see Armstrong [1961], pp. 35–7). But it is not in much dispute that, however it might be mediated, perceptual belief is a normal outcome of perception.

I use the term 'perceptual belief' for a certain kind of belief characteristically gained through perception. It is problematic exactly how this kind of belief is to be

To experience music with musical understanding a listener must perceive various kinds of musical processes, structures and relationships. But to perceive phrasing, cadences and harmonic progressions, for example, does not require the listener to conceptualise them in musical terms. A listener can experience these phenomena whether or not he hears them under the description they are given in a correct analysis of the music. This description applies to the experience of a listener who experiences the music with understanding; but the listener does not need to recognise this fact in order to have the experience it describes.[16]

In other words, the listener can satisfy a psychological description such as 'perceives the chord as a dominant' – that's what it is for the description to "apply" to his experience – without exercising the music-theoretic concept of a dominant; and it is coherent with Budd's view that the listener need not possess that concept at all. This is what, in my terminology, it means to say that the hearing so attributed is weakly nonconceptual: one can satisfy the attribution without possessing the (music-theoretic) concepts contained in the attribution.[17]

But what reason do we have to think that Budd's claim is true? (Nowhere, as far as I can see, does he give a real argument for it.) What are the constraints on concept possession, in particular, such that his thesis follows? It is certainly true that most listeners have

---

defined. Not every belief gained through some perceptual process or other is properly regarded as perceptual: reading in the newspaper that it is hot today in New York does not count as perceiving it. And it is not clear that in perception one always *acquires* a belief: one may perceive something to be red when one already believes it to be red. As a further complication, one may, doubting one's senses, not believe what one perceives. These issues do not affect the present argument, so I suppress them. For discussion, see Armstrong (1968), Pitcher (1971), and Pitson (1990).

[16]Budd (1985), p. 247.

[17]This notion, in different terminology, is found in Crane (1992b), pp. 143, 149. Notice that being weakly nonconceptual is relative to the way it is attributed; the same psychological state might be attributed in different ways, employing different concepts.

never heard of dominant chords, but is that enough to establish his thesis? If it is not (as I shall argue), what does establish it?

I shall argue for a version of Budd's claim that puts the issue, a bit more narrowly, in terms of belief: that it is possible to hear a sound-event as a dominant without having the belief expressed by the sentence 'That is a dominant'.[18] My purpose is to exhibit a kind of musical hearing for which this is true and, more important, to show what is necessary in order to establish it.

As I shall argue, there is also a sense of 'hears a dominant' on which a listener who satisfies that description – typically a trained listener such as a music theorist – normally does have the belief expressed by that sentence. It is prima facie plausible that someone who enjoys this hearing state cannot fail to have that belief. If that is right, then we have thereby captured an important distinction between levels of musical competence: hearing and thought are related by epistemic (i.e, conceptual) equivalence for the trained listener, but not for the ordinary listener. In what follows I shall argue this point, but also point to problems that arise.

The argument that a certain kind of musical hearing is weakly nonconceptual will not, however, count against the belief thesis, since musical hearing's not being a certain *music-theoretic* belief in no way entails that it is not some *other* belief. Only when we get to the argument that musical hearing is *strongly* nonconceptual will the belief thesis be seriously challenged.

At this point, we need a framework for talking about beliefs, contents, and ascriptions. Let me set out some assumptions, most of which will be very familiar and many recognizably Fregean in origin, though freely adapted. I am aware that these assumptions are open to all sorts of challenges.[19] But it is a plausible initial strategy to

---

[18]I shall sometimes call such a belief, expressed by a (music-theoretic) sentence, a *theoretical belief.*

[19]For a recent criticism of Fregean tenets, see Millikan (1991). I was led to focus on considerations of cognitive significance by Peacocke, especially (1989). My thinking about these issues has also been influenced by Jerry Fodor, especially in his semi-

pose the basic issues of musical intentionality in terms of this familiar framework.

Here then are our assumptions. Belief is a relation to *information;* so are certain other psychological states such as doubt, hope, desire, and (in general) thought. Different psychological states may be relations to the same information, for example, believing that Quine is wise and doubting that Quine is wise. All of these relations are instances of *grasping* information. A thought is *informative* to one if and only if the information one grasps in thinking it is different from that of any belief one has.[20] Most important, a rational thinker cannot simultaneously enter into both belief and doubt with respect to the same information.[21]

A belief is individuated by the information one grasps in having the belief. Hence, belief tokens are type-identical if and only if they are a matter of grasping the same information. (Sometimes it is convenient to call such belief tokens epistemically equivalent.)

Sentences present information.[22] (Information is not presented only via sentences, of course; it may be presented perceptually as well.) The belief a sentence expresses is the belief in which one grasps the information it presents.[23] Someone understands a sen-

nar on modes of presentation (City University of New York Graduate Center, Fall 1993). The exposition to follow, and my conception of the issues, owe much to Fodor's discussion.

[20]In my view, our intuitions about informativeness are foundational to our notion of when beliefs are the same or different, and it is best to leave the notion of informativeness as primitive. I thus follow Peacocke (1992b) in this way (I owe this point to Jerry Fodor).

[21]The assumption of rationality is in force throughout this study. Nowhere will it be plausible to impute irrationality to thinkers or listeners. Thus, in effect, I am assuming a notion of belief that requires rational thinkers and agents, or for which rationality is constitutive.

[22]Here I mean declarative sentences. These may include music-theoretic symbolism as well as natural language.

[23]I assume here that there is a unique information value any sentence presents,

tence if upon reading or hearing it, she is able to grasp the information it presents. If someone understands a sentence, then, she has the belief it expresses just in case she is disposed to assent to it (sincerely, in appropriate conditions).

The information a sentence presents is built up of components contributed by certain of its parts. I shall assume that these include singular terms. It is a consequence of a well-known argument by Frege (in connection with "Frege's puzzle") that the components of information contributed by singular terms in this way cannot be their referents, that is, the ordinary objects such terms denote. The argument goes like this. The sentences

(1) The Evening Star is in the sky,
(2) The Morning Star is in the sky

present different information values, since it is possible to believe (1), say, and doubt (2).[24] Hence, in these sentences, 'Evening Star' and 'Morning Star' contribute different components of information. But those terms are coreferential; they both denote the planet Venus. Hence their contributions to information cannot be the same as what they denote, but must be *modes of presentation* of those objects.[25]

By a parallel argument for predicates, we may introduce modes of presentation of *properties*. Here I shall take properties to be *intensions*, functions from possible worlds to sets of objects. The intension of a

and therefore (by the conditions on type identity of belief) any sentence expresses exactly one belief.

[24]This is a variant of the argument in Frege (1980b [1892]), p. 56. One may ask, as Fodor has asked, what supports the claim that the transition from doubting (2) to believing (2) represents the acquisition of new information. It does not seem to me that it is useful to try to found this on something else; there is a sense of 'information' on which it is self-evident that the transition represents the acquisition of new information. Of course, one might mean something else by 'information', as Salmon (1986, p. 78) does, but that does not affect the point.

[25]Frege (1980b [1892]), p. 57. I am indebted to the discussion in Schiffer (1992), pp. 501–3.

predicate is a function that maps each possible world to its extension in that world, which is the set of objects in that world that satisfy the predicate, or of which the predicate is true.[26] Consider

(3) This is an equilateral triangle,
(4) This is an equiangular triangle.

It is possible to believe (3) while doubting (4), or vice versa. So they present different information; yet 'equilateral triangle' has the same intension as 'equiangular triangle'. Hence, their contributions to information value cannot be this common intension; we must say, rather, that they are different modes of presentation of that intension.

Having introduced intensions, we can gain economy by thinking of what modes of presentation present as intensions generally. To a singular term there corresponds an intension that maps each possible world to a singleton set with the denoted object as sole member (or to the null set, in worlds in which the object does not exist). To an entire sentence there corresponds an intension that maps each possible world to a truth value; the information value the sentence pre-

---

[26]The above account is adapted and simplified from Lewis (1983b), pp. 193–5. There, Lewis thinks of intensions, more generally, as mappings from indices to extensions, where a possible world is but one component of an index; other components are sensitive to context in various ways. Such context-dependent components are necessary to account for, among other things, the egocentric nature of perceptual content. I suppress this complication. Whether this simplification is material depends on whether music-theoretic predicates have an indexical component – if, for example, 'tonic' is in relevant ways like 'here' – but for the purposes of the argument to follow, I wish to avoid such complications. Another difference with Lewis's views is that Lewis identifies properties not with intensions, but with sets of possible objects (1983, p. 135); again, this difference will not be crucial.

The present invocation of intensions and possible worlds is one un-Fregean aspect to the account (nowhere, as far as I know, are these notions anticipated by Frege). But it is not un-Fregean to suppose that properties – construed here as intensions – have modes of presentation.

sents is (in turn) a mode of presentation of that intension. Believing may be thought of in general, then, as a relation to an intension under a mode of presentation.

A *content* is an object of belief. There are different levels of content, corresponding to different kinds of things one may take a belief to be directed toward. Thus far we have seen two levels, information values (i.e., modes of presentation) and intensions. Intuitively speaking, different levels of content correspond to more or less mediate objects of belief.[27] Whether additional levels have to be postulated is something we shall investigate.

A *concept* is a certain psychological capacity, an ability to have beliefs (and thoughts generally) in which one grasps a particular mode of presentation.[28] A concept is individuated, then, by the corresponding mode of presentation.

There is more to say about beliefs. I am broadly in sympathy with a functionalistic view of beliefs and mental states generally, on which such states are defined in terms of their causal roles. However, the argument of this chapter does not depend on such a view, and so it would be premature to introduce it now.

To turn now to belief *ascriptions*. A belief ascription specifies a certain kind of belief and says that someone has it; crucially, the kind of belief thus specified may be different from a *type* as previously defined (where type identity is determined by identity of mode of presentation). Let me explain.

We call a sentence of the form 'S believes that p' an *ascription sentence*; its corresponding *content sentence* is 'p'. (For example, to the ascription sentence 'Sam believes that Quine is wise' there corresponds the content sentence 'Quine is wise'.) I will say that an ascription is mode-of-presentation-preserving, or m.p.-preserving for

---

[27] I owe this notion of mediacy in objects of belief to Curtis Brown (1992).

[28] This notion of a concept as a capacity is derived from Armstrong (1968), pp. 339–40, and (1973), pp. 50–2. It is different from that of Frege's use of *Begriff* (1980a [1892], p. 42) and from Peacocke's use of 'concept' to mean a mode of presentation of a property (1989, p. 316n).

short, if, in order to satisfy the ascription, one must have the belief expressed by its content sentence, that is, a belief with the same information value; otherwise, the ascription is non-m.p.-preserving. A true m.p.-preserving belief ascription will satisfy the following *disquotational principle:* if someone satisfies a true m.p.-preserving ascription and understands its content sentence, then she will be disposed to assent to the latter.[29] There is no such requirement on non-m.p.-preserving ascriptions.

By way of illustration, consider a sentence that may be read either as m.p.-preserving or non-m.p.-preserving:

(5) Sam believes that the chairman's husband will call.[30]

This sentence admits of two natural readings, only one of which is m.p.-preserving. The m.p.-preserving reading requires that, if Sam is an English speaker, he is disposed to assent to 'The chairman's husband will call', whereas the other says, more or less, that there is someone such that Sam believes he will call and such that he is the chairman's husband. The first reading requires, in other words, that Sam be appropriately related to the mode of presentation expressed by 'the chairman's husband', whereas the second does not. Non-m.p.-preserving ascription, then, does not pick out a belief type in the sense defined earlier; it induces a different taxonomy.

The distinction between m.p.-preserving and non-m.p.-preserving ascriptions runs along similar lines as, but is not exactly equivalent to, the familiar distinction between referentially opaque and referentially transparent ascriptions.[31] In referentially transparent ascriptions, coreferential expressions (i.e., ones that have the same denotation in ordinary contexts) may be substituted for one another *salva veritate;* in opaque ascriptions they may not. As it happens, these

---

[29]This is one-half of the strengthened disquotational principle in Kripke (1988 [1979]), p. 113.

[30]Adapted from an example of Jerry Fodor's (in a lecture).

[31]On referentially opaque and transparent ascriptions, see Quine (1966 [1956]).

distinctions tend to run together: ordinarily, ascriptions are opaque just in case they are m.p.-preserving and transparent just in case they are not. But since even a single instance of substitution failure is sufficient for opacity, the latter is obviously a weaker condition than being m.p.-preserving; and for our purposes, what is important is whether an ascription is m.p.-preserving, not whether it is opaque.

How are belief ascriptions related to contents? A belief ascription specifies a certain kind of belief by designating a content that individuates that kind. Different belief ascriptions may specify contents at different levels. For an m.p.-preserving ascription, the level specified is the mode of presentation.[32] For a referentially transparent ascription (which is the typical case of a non-m.p.-preserving ascription) it is an ordinary object (person, planet) or, more generally, an intension. (At bottom, contents are whatever has to be postulated in order to give a satisfactory semantic account of belief ascriptions, on the assumption that the latter refer to those contents.)

2.4 To return to the musical case. In view of the foregoing, the central questions for us can now be formulated thus: How are the cognitive states ascribed by hearing ascriptions related in content to the beliefs expressed by the corresponding content sentences? What levels of content do they share? Are different kinds of musical hearing different in these respects?

By way of answering these questions, let me start by carrying out the argument that a certain kind of musical hearing is weakly nonconceptual, which, from the present standpoint, means that that kind of hearing is epistemically inequivalent to the belief expressed by the content sentence corresponding to the ascription of that hearing.[33] The relevant kind of hearing will be that described on the rel-

---

[32]This is Frege's dictum that "in indirect speech . . . words do not have their customary meaning but designate what is usually their sense" (1980b [1892] ["On Sense and Meaning"], p. 59).

[33]Again, we should note that being weakly nonconceptual is a property of a state relative to an ascription, i.e., a way of describing that state.

ative chroma model. What needs to be shown, then, is that it is possible for someone to satisfy 'S hears x as a $\hat{5}$' (for example) without having the belief expressed by 'x is a $\hat{5}$'.[34]

First – to show what is at stake – an argument that *doesn't* work. Suppose we have a listener who has never heard of chroma, $\hat{5}$, and so forth. The chroma theory is intended to apply to this sort of listener, at least in certain circumstances, so let us suppose that such circumstances obtain and hence that our listener hears a certain pitch, x, as a $\hat{5}$. Since he knows no theory, he will not assent to 'x is a $\hat{5}$'. Is this enough to establish that he does not have the belief expressed by 'x is a $\hat{5}$'? No: no more than a monolingual English speaker's lack of inclination to assent to 'Der Schnee ist weiss' is enough to establish that he does not believe what the German sentence expresses, or that the latter has an information value distinct from that of the English sentence 'Snow is white'. Lack of disposition to assent establishes nothing by itself; what we need is a case in which someone who *understands* the sentence is not disposed to assent to it, and so far we do not have such a case.

But, it may be objected, doesn't the fact that one state is perceptual and the other linguistically mediated entail that the two are not epistemically equivalent? No, because a difference in *medium*, or modality, does not necessarily make for a difference in information grasped, any more than does a difference in language.

So far, then, we have seen no real argument for Budd's claim that the ordinary listener does not possess music-theoretic concepts such as $\hat{5}$. True, he cannot use that term to express the concept. But neither can a monolingual English speaker use 'Schnee' to express his concept of snow, yet it does not follow that he fails to possess the concept the term expresses.

---

[34]To forestall a possible misunderstanding: aspects of content corresponding to 'x' are not at issue in what follows. The question is what component of content is contributed by predicates such as '$\hat{5}$'. I assume that listener and ascribers alike use 'x' as a name for the relevant sound-event and that no problems of reidentification arise in that connection.

What is needed is an analogue of a Frege case (like 'Evening Star' and 'Morning Star') in which there is both *belief* and *doubt*: hearing a sound-event x as a $\hat{5}$ and having the appropriate relation of doubt toward the sentence 'x is a $\hat{5}$' (which requires understanding). Having such doubt entails that one does not have the belief expressed by the sentence, and, therefore, whatever hearing a sound-event as a $\hat{5}$ is, it cannot be that belief.

Here is such a case. Imagine a sophomore music theory student taking an ear training test. Her task is to label the pitches of a tonal passage she hears with scalestep numbers in the key of the passage. Since her ear-training skills are only average, she does not always know the right answer. So there is some pitch x – a $\hat{5}$, say – such that she is in doubt as to whether it is a $\hat{5}$; she is not disposed to assent to 'x is a $\hat{5}$'.

I call this sort of listener an *intermediate listener* (what it is intermediate between will become apparent).[35] For our listener, 'x is a $\hat{5}$' is informative; when her instructor tells her, 'That was a $\hat{5}$', it is a genuine "extension of her knowledge," a belief she did not already possess.

At the same time, the chroma theory is supposed to apply to our listener. (Sometimes the chroma theory is restricted to the recognition of familiar melodies, but inability to label scale degrees can occur even there.) Hence, assuming the theory is true, our student hears x as a $\hat{5}$. So we have a case in which someone hears x as a $\hat{5}$ without having the belief expressed by 'x is a $\hat{5}$'. Therefore, whatever that state of hearing is, it cannot be that belief.[36] (Moreover, it is not

[35]The notion is relative to a predicate: a listener S is an intermediate listener with respect to F just in case S understands 'F' but, normally, when S hears some sound-event x as an F, S is not disposed to assent to 'x is an F'.

[36]It might be objected that the intermediate listener does not genuinely understand '$\hat{5}$' because she cannot identify instances of $\hat{5}$ by ear. But surely this is too strong a condition on understanding, since then no one could understand the chroma theory itself without having that aural ability. This is implausible: psychologists do not have to have that perceptual skill in order to pose and understand the model.

some relation to the relevant mode of presentation *other* than belief: though we sometimes have reason to speak of different attitudes toward the same information – believing that p, doubting that p, hoping that p – in view of rational and inferential connections between such attitudes, there is no such reason here.)

As the reader will note, nothing has been said so far to refute the belief thesis. It seems entirely open to say that hearing a pitch as a $\hat{5}$ is some perceptual belief or other, so long as it is type-distinct – involves grasping a different mode of presentation – from that expressed by 'x is a $\hat{5}$'. ('S hears x as $\hat{5}$' would then simply be a non-m.p.-preserving belief ascription.)

2.5   There is an analogy between the intermediate listener's situation and that described in Molyneux's question. As Locke, to whom William Molyneux posed the question, recounts it:

Suppose a Man born blind, and now adult, and taught by his touch to distinguish between a Cube, and a Sphere of the same metal, and nighly of the same bigness, so as to tell, when he felt one and t'other, which is the Cube, which the Sphere. Suppose then the Cube and Sphere placed on a Table, and the Blind Man to be made to see. Quaere, Whether by his sight, before he touch'd them, he could now distinguish, and tell, which is the Globe, which the Cube.

Locke reports that Molyneux answered the question in the negative, a verdict with which Locke himself agrees.[37]

The intermediate listener's situation is analogous to a negative outcome to Molyneux's question: sight is to touch in the Molyneux case as hearing is to reading music in the listener's case. Our listener's ability to identify scale degrees upon reading music (which I assume she has) is parallel to the ability of Molyneux's man to identify shapes by touch; our listener's inability to identify scale degrees by

---

[37]Locke (1975 [1700]), II.ix.8, p. 146, italics omitted.

ear is parallel to the newly sighted man's inability to identify shapes by looking at them.

In an illuminating essay, Gareth Evans has argued that what is at stake in Molyneux's question is how conceptual abilities are individuated and related to one another. As Evans sees it, the main issue is whether "there is a unitary conceptual ability associated in the case of most adults with the word 'square' – mastery of a single concept" or, instead, "the sighted adult's use of the word 'square' rests upon two separable and conceptually unconnected abilities."[38] A positive outcome – in which the newly sighted man is able to identify the shapes – is consistent with the hypothesis that he is exercising such a unitary conceptual capacity, a concept of *square* to which there are both visual and tactile inputs, so to speak. A negative outcome entails that the man has no such unitary ability, and – if it is correct to speak of concepts in connection with both touch and sight in this case – that there are two distinct concepts at work here, *tangible square* and *visible square*.[39] In the musical case, then, the inability of the intermediate listener to identify scale degrees demonstrates that theoretical concepts and perception do *not* converge here on a unitary conceptual ability.

What would be an example in which language and perception do converge? Ordinary shape concepts, for one: when one sees an object as round, one is not apt to find 'That's round' informative.[40] And, quite plausibly, that is because, in seeing an object as round, one grasps the same information as is expressed by 'round'. Of course, it can always be argued that the modes of presentation are

[38]Evans (1985), pp. 373–4. In what follows, I simplify Evans's exposition of the issues.

[39]However, I do not see that anything follows from this about normal sighted adults: they may well have the relevant kind of unitary ability. The situation is asymmetrical in that a positive outcome, though not a negative one, has implications for normal sighted adults.

[40]Assuming one takes one's experience at face value, i.e., does not doubt one's senses.

distinct and that we infer one thing from another, but there is no reason to adopt this more complicated explanation.

Is there a kind of musical hearing for which perception and theory converge on a "unitary conceptual ability"? Quite plausibly, this is the kind of hearing characteristic of the music analyst. If a Schenkerian analyst hears a passage as a dominant prolongation, he will normally be disposed to assent to the sentence 'This is a dominant prolongation' (if he speaks English). I call this sort of listener an *expert listener*.[41] Typically, of course, someone is an expert listener by virtue of perceptual training.

It is plausible to understand the case of the expert listener as one in which, given his hearing of a passage as a dominant prolongation, the sentence 'This is a dominant prolongation' is uninformative to him. It is plausible, then, to analyze the ascription 'He hears this as a dominant prolongation' as ascribing a belief type-identical to – having the same mode of presentation as – the former sentence. This sort of hearing ascription would then be, in contrast to ascriptions about the ordinary or intermediate listener, m.p.-preserving.

As another example, consider the sense in which a student may be said to learn to "hear" intervals or scale degrees. Someone who satisfies this sort of ascription – 'She is hearing (that as) a perfect fifth' – is typically disposed to assent to the corresponding content sentence – 'That's a perfect fifth'. Again, it is plausible to understand the case as one in which hearing and belief converge on a unitary conceptual ability.

I have not, to be sure, given a conclusive argument that these cases should be analyzed in terms of identity of belief. The fact that the listener is disposed to assent to the relevant theoretical sentence might be explained, instead, as an inference on the subject's part: she might be inferring the theoretical belief from what she hears. But

---

[41]Again, the notion is relative to a predicate: a listener S is an expert listener with respect to F just in case S understands 'F' and, normally, whenever S hears a sound-event x as an F, S is disposed to assent to 'x is an F'.

we would need a reason to adopt this more complicated explanation; whether there is such a reason is an issue we will take up later.

For now, let us say provisionally that two kinds of hearing ascriptions may be distinguished: one whereby the kind of hearing ascribed is type-distinct – involves a different mode of presentation – from the belief expressed by the content sentence, and one where hearing and belief are type-identical. Let us call the former *theory-inequivalent hearing* and the latter *theory-equivalent hearing* (indicating epistemic equivalence, or lack thereof, to a theoretical belief).[42] This points to an important distinction between levels of musical competence. Whereas a relatively untrained (e.g., intermediate) listener has, in hearing and linguistically mediated theoretical belief, "two separable and conceptually unconnected abilities," the relevant aural training brings about an integrated faculty embracing hearing and linguistically mediated belief.[43]

Theory-equivalent hearing is then typically integrated with linguistically mediated thought, and theory-inequivalent hearing typi-

[42]Note that theory equivalence is a property of a type of hearing under a description. The theory-equivalent/theory-inequivalent distinction is essentially the same as that between m.p.-preserving and non-m.p.-preserving hearing ascriptions, except that one applies to states, the other to ascriptions.

[43]In respect of this sort of perceptual and cognitive integration, the expert listener's relation to the intermediate listener is something like that of ordinary sighted people to patients with perceptual deficits such as visual agnosia; see Zeki (1993), pp. 309–19.

Two observations. First, the point in the text does not depend on the relevant faculty being an outcome of training; it might just as well be innate. Second, ordinary listeners might well have certain concepts that enter into their hearing as attributed by hearing ascriptions, e.g., strong and weak beats, or *crescendo*. It may be that the ordinary concepts of *strong* and *weak* enter into an ordinary listener's perception in such a way that the listener cannot hear beats as strong or weak without finding the labeling of them as such uninformative. And it is hard to imagine that anyone who understands the term 'crescendo' can hear a passage as containing a crescendo but be in doubt as to whether the term applies. In cases like this, an ordinary listener may already be an "expert" with respect to the relevant music-theoretic properties.

cally is not. But why should there be these two rather different levels of psychological description? How do they function differently?

The ascription of theory-inequivalent hearing typically occurs in a context of psychological explanation, where the goal is to identify what it is the listener detects. Such ascriptions are typically third-person. Of course, someone who has a command of the language can make such an ascription about himself as well, but what is significant is that he has no privileged epistemic access to these relevant facts; his disposition to assent to such an ascription is not evidence for it, and a disposition to dissent or express doubt is not evidence against it.

The ascription of theory-equivalent hearing, in contrast, is characteristically first-person. In this context, the function is one not of psychological explanation but of communication. The analyst wants to share a (perhaps idiosyncratic) hearing of a passage with others who speak her language; they may want to try that hearing on for size and perhaps come to appreciate the music in a new way. Such first-person ascriptions are like *avowals*, such as 'That looks red'.[44] They have a different epistemic status from theory-inequivalent ascriptions: the fact that a music analyst says he hears a passage in a certain way constitutes prima facie evidence that he hears it that way, much as with ordinary perceptual avowals.[45] (It is defeasible evidence, but evidence nonetheless.) And conversely, dissent or expressing doubt constitutes evidence that he does not hear it in that way. Theory-equivalent hearing is, in short, integrated into the language game of avowal and ascription in a way much different from theory-inequivalent hearing.

Hence, different notions of mental representation are generated by these different sorts of ascriptions. What is more, it is an open, empirical question – the answer to which may be different in different cases – how the psychological states that underlie theory-equiva-

---

[44]On avowals, see Ryle (1949), p. 102.
[45]The issue of epistemic authority is raised by Cumming (1992), p. 355.

lent hearing are related to those underlying theory-inequivalent hearing. It is an open question whether the psychological state the trained listener is in when she hears a pitch as a $\hat{5}$ is the same state as the untrained listener's chroma representation of $\hat{5}$ – differing only in its *relations* to linguistic capacities – or a different state entirely. Moreover, if those states are distinct, it is an open question whether there is a close enough connection between them that the trained listener's reports about her hearing provide us with evidence about the states of the untrained listener. I do not pretend to know the answer to these questions, but certainly there is no a priori reason to think that the answer to any of them is yes; the burden of proof is to show that it is.

Perhaps I am making too much of this point, but I am not sure that the distinction between theory-equivalent and theory-inequivalent hearing has always been fully appreciated in music-theoretic circles. An example is provided by two ways of looking at GTTM's representations, which are not always separated but should be. In GTTM itself, the authors' "intuitions" about the structure of particular passages are treated as a reliable source of information about the representations of experienced listeners who do not know the theory.[46] At the same time, there has been interest in testing experimentally whether such listeners have representations along lines described in GTTM, where in those experimental paradigms such states function as explanatory constructs in connection with the production of musical behavior.[47] But what ensures that they are talking about the same thing? Why should theorists' verbally accessible "in-

[46]That this is an implicit assumption of GTTM is shown by, e.g., the authors' straightforward statement of "correct grouping structures" (Lerdahl and Jackendoff [1983], p. 14). It is clear from the context that "correct" here means "true of the experienced listener's representation," where that listener may not know the theory (p. 3).

[47]E.g., Bigand et al. (1993) and Dibben (1993); see also references cited in Jackendoff (1987), p. 239.

tuitions" necessarily converge on the same psychological states as those explanatory constructs? Could they perhaps be different states, described homonymously? The fact that the same music-theoretic term is used in each does not ensure that 'hears as (such-and-such)' is univocal, or refers to the same psychological state, any more than the fact that we identify both a picture of Churchill and a thought about Churchill via the term 'Churchill' makes picture and thought the same. When the operational definitions for the relevant ascriptions are different, there is no reason to assume that they point to the same thing.

A related issue. Lerdahl and Jackendoff make much of the point that their theory is modeled after generative linguistics, but GTTM's reliance for data on theorists' intuitions about structure has no counterpart, as far as I know, in linguistic theory. As I understand linguistic methodology (and I am open to correction) the intuitions that serve as their data do not get much more theory-laden than saying whether or not a sentence is grammatical: they do not include intuitions about syntactic structure in the way GTTM's data include intuitions about musical structure.[48] This is not to deny that linguists, or for that matter speakers untrained in linguistics, have some intuitions about syntactic structure; it is just to say that such intuitions do not have a central evidential or confirmatory role in syntactic theory.[49] This is because linguists do not assume that the structures they want to theorize about are consciously available. Intuitions about musical structure play a much different theoretical role in GTTM;

[48]I have in mind here theories such as those described in Chomsky (1957) and (1965).

[49]Some linguists take an extreme skeptical or eliminativist position: Robert Friedin, in conversation, stated the view that no one has any intuitions about linguistic structure. Though I do not agree with this position, it is easy to see why there is much to recommend it as a methodological precept.

I am indebted to Christopher Peacocke for a discussion of these issues. On speakers' intuitions about linguistic structure (with an analogy to perception), see also Stich (1971), p. 494.

hence, the analogy between GTTM and generative grammar is not as strong as Lerdahl and Jackendoff suggest.[50]

2.6   In order to characterize a distinction between levels of musical competence, I have appealed to the distinction between theory-equivalent and theory-inequivalent hearing. I would like to briefly compare this approach with some alternatives.

One such alternative is predicated on the difference between 'knowing *how*' versus 'knowing *that*'. Leonard Meyer has aptly suggested that understanding music, at a level we associate with the ordinary listener, is more like knowing how to ride a bicycle than knowing a theory about bicycle riding.[51] A related distinction is that between "procedural" and "declarative" knowledge. Declarative knowledge, as the music psychologist W. Jay Dowling explains it, is something to which one has conscious verbal access, whereas procedural knowledge is a matter of knowing *how*.[52]

The problem with appealing to knowing *how* in this connection, however, is that most, if not all, of the ascriptions we are attempting to interpret are meant to attribute a *representational* faculty to the listener. One typically appeals to knowing *how* in order to *avoid* making a representational claim. But that is a strategy we cannot adopt if – as on much contemporary cognitive theory – our model of the mind is a representational one.

It should be apparent, moreover, that Dowling's dichotomy is not exhaustive: knowing *how* is not the only alternative to verbally acces-

---

[50]Although it is natural to attempt to draw an analogy between music theory and linguistics (see Sloboda [1985], ch. 2), there are important disanalogies as well. There is no real counterpart in linguistics to the "expert listener." And in music we are more interested in the structures of particular pieces than linguists are interested in the structures of particular sentences (for their own sake). Marantz (1985) argues that music theory bears a stronger analogy in some ways to literary theory than to linguistics.

[51]Meyer (1973), p. 16. On the distinction between knowing *how* and knowing *that,* see Ryle (1949), ch. 2. For a relevant discussion, see Polanyi (1962), ch. 5.

[52]Dowling (1993b), p. 7.

sible knowing *that*. There can be mental representation (*that* such-and-such is the case) that the subject cannot put into words; that is precisely the sort of cognition characteristic of the ordinary listener. An appeal to knowing *how*, then, misses the mark.

A second notion, often appealed to in order to characterize the ordinary listener, is that of unconscious cognition. There are three main reasons to avoid this approach: the notion of the unconscious is obscure, so it serves more as a label for the problem than an explication; the phenomena (thus far at least) can be explained more economically in terms of informational relations or modes of presentation; and insofar as we do understand the notion of consciousness, it is evident that aspects of musical perception sometimes alleged to be unconscious are in fact conscious (on any ordinary understanding of the term).

Of course, the notion of a mode of presentation brings with it its share of obscurity, too, but we would have those problems anyway: we will always have Hesperus and Phosphorus.[53] And it clears some mystery away from the musical case when we see that much of what we are trying to explain boils down to the sorts of problems of information epitomized by Hesperus and Phosphorus rather than to much vaguer issues of consciousness. Listeners' inabilities to label what they hear in music-theoretic terms provide no more reason to postulate anything unconscious than does, say, a disinclination on the part of the ancients to assent to 'The Evening Star is in the sky' while gazing at it in the morning. We have seen, therefore, no reason to invoke the notion of the unconscious.

Given an ordinary understanding of the term 'conscious', moreover, it seems very problematic to say that aspects of music perception alleged to be unconscious are in fact so. (Certainly the burden of proof is to show that they are, since listening to music is a full-blown conscious experience if there ever was one.) In this connection it is helpful to refer to Jackendoff's treatment of the issues. Jackendoff

[53]The Evening Star and the Morning Star, and the ensuing puzzles about belief.

has claimed that the levels of representation in GTTM other than the musical surface – the grouping, metrical, time-span, and prolongational levels – are all unconscious. Jackendoff states, for example, that "one does not experience four simultaneous hierarchies while listening to music."[54] And elsewhere he writes that the goal of GTTM is "to address the formal organization that experienced listeners *unconsciously attribute* to a piece of music and the principles by which they determine this organization."[55]

Jackendoff distinguishes several senses of the dichotomy between 'conscious' and 'unconscious', separating his usage from others. He explicitly disavows any sense of 'conscious' on which one must be able to report what one is conscious of in words. And he does not identify consciousness with *self*-consciousness, the reflective awareness that one is conscious of something. For Jackendoff, the notion of consciousness is bound up, rather, with that of "experience"; it is part of what he calls the "phenomenological mind."[56] If I understand him right, Jackendoff thinks of conscious experience along the lines of those who speak of what "it is like" to have this or that experience.[57]

But given this disavowal of a verbal reportability criterion for consciousness and the acceptance of a phenomenological one, it is rather puzzling why Jackendoff should claim that the kind of perception outlined in GTTM is unconscious. For this musical perception clearly has the required phenomenological salience. Consider an analogy with visual grouping, as Lerdahl and Jackendoff themselves suggest (Example 2.6).[58] In each case, the musical passage is similar

[54]Jackendoff (1987), p. 293.

[55]Ibid., p. 214, emphasis mine. It is clear from this that what is said to be unconscious is the attribution of organization, not just the principles that govern it; and I take this to mean that the listener is not conscious of the organization he attributes, not just that he is not conscious *of attributing* it.

[56]Ibid., pp. 3–7.

[57]Nagel (1974).

[58]Lerdahl and Jackendoff (1983), pp. 40–2; Example 2.6 is reproduced from p. 42.

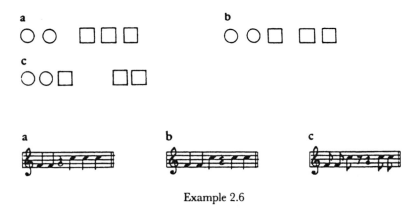

Example 2.6

in its grouping properties to the corresponding visual pattern. The analogy is apt, but surely it is incorrect to say that the perception of visual grouping is unconscious in these cases. When an aspect switch occurs in visual grouping, that change is as phenomenologically robust as anyone could want. Moreover, we could not recognize the similarity between the visual and musical examples without being aware of similar properties in each.

Again, tension and relaxation, or weak and strong beats – part and parcel of GTTM's prolongational and metrical levels, respectively – are phenomenally present in music: they are features we experience, with as full-fledged a phenomenal character as colors and shapes. By Jackendoff's own criterion, then, such cognition is conscious. Of course, many listeners cannot *report* those aspects of their musical experience in GTTM's (or perhaps any) terms, but Jackendoff has already ruled out verbal reportability as a criterion. Likewise, listeners may not be reflectively aware *that* they are hearing a passage that sounds a certain way; but Jackendoff has disavowed this sense too.[59]

---

[59]Sometimes one listens to music in the way one drives along a road automatically (for this notion of "unconscious perception" see Armstrong [1968], pp. 231–2). But surely that is a side issue; the problems of characterizing musical experience do not dissolve when we focus on listening with full attention.

A further problem: on any ordinary understanding of 'conscious', verbal reportability is a sufficient condition of consciousness (even if, as Jackendoff stipulates, it is not a necessary condition). But then the very existence of GTTM becomes inexplicable. How can the theory have been discovered, given the authors' methodology, if the states it describes are unconscious? The problem here is not with the rule systems, but with representations of particular passages heard on particular occasions. If such representations are unconscious, how is it that anyone – including the authors of GTTM – knows what content his own representations have, and is able to report this?[60]

Jackendoff's answer to this question is, at best, perplexing. He says we have access to such facts through "intuition": "our unconscious understanding of music enables us intuitively to choose a hierarchical segmentation."[61] But surely this is wanting to eat one's cake and have it too: any understanding that one can put into words or symbols is ipso facto conscious. Of course, it is open to Jackendoff to say that representations that are *ordinarily* unconscious can sometimes be made conscious, and reported. But Jackendoff nowhere takes this line explicitly; and even if he were to do so, we would then need an account of what the mechanism is by which unconscious representations are made conscious and – more important – why we have reason to think that that mechanism is reliable. We would need, in other words, an account of how we know that the listener is not simply acquiring *new* beliefs by this process, as opposed to revealing the contents of representations she already has.[62]

---

[60]Actually, it is not strictly correct to claim verbal reportability as a sufficient condition for consciousness. There are marginal examples to the contrary, such as blindsight; see Weiskrantz (1988), p. 187. But I doubt that anyone would want to claim that knowledge of GTTM is akin to blindsight.

[61]Jackendoff (1987), p. 219.

[62]Let me stress that I am not airing a general worry about the validity or usefulness of notions of unconscious representation in psychology. My point is simply that, given GTTM's actual methodology, the representations it is telling us about must be, in any ordinary sense, conscious.

For these reasons, the notion of unconscious cognition is – as far as we can see up to this point – of little explanatory value, if not outright wrong, as applied to music perception.

There is one other notion the relevance of which I want to consider, which is Stephen Stich's conception of a *subdoxastic state*.[63] The main requirements on subdoxastic states are that they are unconscious and that they lack inferential integration. Since I have already discussed the issue of consciousness, let me turn to inferential integration.

An example of failure of inferential integration would be a situation in which a linguist believes an incorrect psychological theory of syntax.[64] In such a case, the linguist might subdoxastically represent certain rules of English inconsistent with those of his theory, or subdoxastically represent the syntactic structure of a sentence in a way inconsistent with the way he thinks of it as having a syntactic structure. There is, however, no inferential mechanism by which he can detect such inconsistency. There is, then, a failure of his subdoxastic representations to integrate inferentially with his theoretical beliefs. And that is, on Stich's conception, one important contrast between what he is calling subdoxastic states and beliefs.

I would readily agree that what I have been describing is a certain failure of inferential integration: of hearing with music-theoretic belief. Let me say, however, that I do not see failure of integration as an especially exotic phenomenon. Failure of integration occurs whenever representations share meaning at a level that is inferentially inert; and that has been around as long as Hesperus and Phosphorus. It is precisely the role of modes of presentation to account for inferential integration of beliefs, or the lack thereof. I see no reason, then, to think of music cognition as subdoxastic in any sense in which subdoxastic states are *opposed* to beliefs, that is, in which they are taken to be something other than beliefs, as Stich seems to want. No such

[63]Stich (1978). In what follows I am indebted to the discussion in Fodor (1983), pp. 83–6.
[64]An example along these lines is given by Stich (1978), p. 508.

reason has, at any rate, been adduced so far; but we will explore this further in the next chapter.

2.7   One loose end. What notion of content is induced by ascriptions of theory-inequivalent hearing? To what sort of entity do they ascribe a relation?[65]

The prima facie plausible answer is that content here is an intension, for the reason that the relevant ascriptions are referentially transparent.[66] But such is not the case, at least not always. There are (theory-inequivalent) contexts in which cointensional predicates are not intersubstitutable *salva veritate*, in other words, where, for predicates *F* and *G* having the same intension, (6) is true and (7) false:

(6) *S* hears *x* as *F*,
(7) *S* hears *x* as *G*.

For an example, it is convenient to consider a passage – or sound-event rather – that is metrically ambiguous, such as Mitsuko Uchida's recorded performance of the opening bars of Mozart's Fantasia in D Minor, K. 397.[67] That sound-event may be heard in terms of a triple subdivision of the beat, or duple (Example 2.7a, b). One can hear it in one way without hearing it in the other (in fact, it seems impossible to hear both at once).[68] But these ways of hearing the passage are satisfied by exactly the same possible sound-events.[69]

---

[65]I emphasize that the discussion to follow is about theory-*in*equivalent hearing. I take it for granted that ascriptions of theory-equivalent hearing are m.p.-preserving and are to be analyzed as Frege does: as designating a mode of presentation.

[66]By analogy, Armstrong (1973), p. 26, suggests that the attribution of beliefs to animals is referentially transparent.

[67]Philips recording 412123-2 PH. The ambiguity I am about to describe is not a peculiarity of this performance or performer, but is also evident in Mieczyslaw Horszowski's recording (Elektra/Nonesuch 79160-2).

[68]I am assuming here that there are theory-inequivalent ways of describing these ways of hearing the passage.

[69]This might be disputed; as Gideon Rosen has pointed out (in conversation), meter may induce certain illusions of greater intensity or loudness on metrically ac-

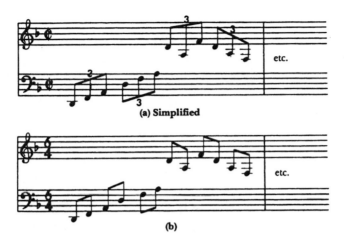

(a) Simplified

(b)

Example 2.7

Hence, the difference between those ways of hearing the passage cannot be captured in terms of intensions, since they have the same intension.

As a second example, let us turn again to the relative chroma model. On that model, a listener represents a pitch in terms of its chroma relative to some reference point, or, in music-theoretic terms, its scale degree with reference to some tonic note. But the same pitch may be referred to more than one tonic: G is scale degree $\hat{5}$ in C as well as $\hat{1}$ in G. Since any pitch that is $\hat{5}$ in C is $\hat{1}$ in G and vice versa, '$\hat{5}$ in C' is cointensional with '$\hat{1}$ in G'.[70] But as the chroma

cented notes, and then the hearings may not turn out to be intensionally equivalent. But while this may be true of meter, I do not think it is true of grouping in general. So at most we would have to find a better example, one not prey to these illusions of meter.

[70]A complication. There is a sense, belonging to music theory, in which '$\hat{5}$ in C' and '$\hat{1}$ in G' are not cointensional, but in which they mean something like 'functioning as $\hat{5}$ in C' and 'functioning as $\hat{1}$ in G', respectively; see Chapter 6. But *that* sense is not that entailed in the psychological theory of chroma representation; the chroma

theory dictates, one may hear a pitch as $\hat{5}$ in C without hearing it as $\hat{1}$ in G. So the difference is again not to be found in that common intension.

The contents proper to hearing ascriptions cannot be intensions; they are too coarse. But as we learned from the example of the intermediate listener, modes of presentation are too fine: whatever that listener is related to in virtue of hearing a pitch as $\hat{5}$, it is not the mode of presentation expressed by '$\hat{5}$', since under that mode of presentation he doubts that the pitch is $\hat{5}$.

What we need is an intermediate level of content, one between, as it were, intensions and modes of presentation. I call this level of content the *structure*. This is a level of content shared by hearing and theoretical belief. (Otherwise, why would we use *those* words to describe that hearing?) Hearing a pitch as $\hat{5}$ in C has the same content, then, at the level of structure, but not the same mode of presentation, as the theoretical belief that the pitch is $\hat{5}$ in C. Of course, those states share content at the level of the intension too, but so do other states that do not correspond to that structure – for example, the theoretical belief that the pitch is $\hat{1}$ in G.[71] These relationships are summarized by the diagram in Example 2.8.

What sort of entities should we take such structures to be? Let me suggest that some sort of set-theoretic construct, built up out of intensions, might play the role of such structures. Thus, the structure corresponding to '$\hat{5}$ in C', for example, might have elements corresponding to the pitch class C and the chroma $\hat{5}$; it would be a structure distinct from, but cointensional with, that corresponding to '$\hat{1}$ in

theory says that a listener has a representation of chroma distance, not of function. And even if it were the latter, all that would be necessary to establish the present point is a context in which some pitch is ambiguous, e.g., a pitch analyzable either as $\hat{5}$ in C or $\hat{1}$ in G. A bridge passage would furnish such an example.

[71]The notion of content I am calling the structure is akin to, but was developed independently of, Peacocke's notion of protopropositional content. See Peacocke (1992a), p. 119.

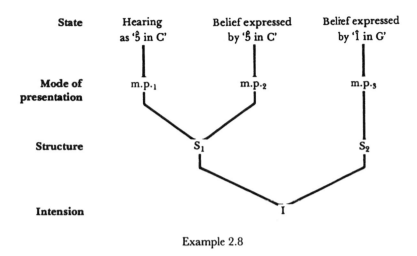

Example 2.8

G'. (Exactly how this is done does not seem a crucial issue; my purpose here is not to suggest a particular candidate for this kind of content but to point out the need for such a level.)

There has been much interest in the issue of how finely grained the contents of intentional states have to be: in particular, whether intensions can do the work of contents – a coarse-grained conception – or whether something that runs finer than necessary equivalence has to be postulated. Robert Stalnaker has argued for a coarse-grained conception of content:

It is essential to rational activities such as deliberation and investigation that the participants represent alternative possibilities, and it is essential to the role of beliefs and desires in the explanation of action that the contents of those attitudes distinguish between the alternative possibilities. The particular ways in which alternative possibilities are represented, or the particular means by which distinctions between them are made, are not essential to such activities and explanations, even if it is essential that the possibilities be represented, and the distinctions be made, in some way or other.[72]

[72]Stalnaker (1984), p. 23.

The point of the present argument is that the kind of content we need to account satisfactorily for musical perception must admit of distinctions finer-grained than Stalnaker allows. Musical perception represents an object as structured in a certain way, and that cuts finer than possibilities; and I suspect, though I cannot undertake to show here, that perception generally has this structural element.[73]

There are, to be sure, standard puzzles that the defender of a coarse-grained conception must deal with, and it is relevant to ask whether Stalnaker's strategy for dealing with them would also apply to the musical case. One of the purest alleged counterexamples is that of mathematical belief. Consider:

(8) $2 + 2 = 4$
(9) $322 - 5 = 317$.

(8) and (9) have the same intension, since they are both necessarily true, but it is possible to believe one and not the other.

Stalnaker's solution to the problem of mathematical belief is, essentially, to let the work be done by sentential attitudes: to characterize the different mathematical beliefs here as beliefs about *sentences*.[74] That seems a fairly plausible solution to the problem of mathematical belief. But it will not work in the case of musical hearing. For the ordinary listener has *no* relevant sentential attitudes, that is, attitudes toward music-theoretic structural descriptions. (And any sentential attitudes the intermediate listener has are irrelevant, since she may just as well be inclined to accept as reject a structural description that correctly characterizes her hearing.)

Musical cognition is thus in a way like thought, in that it requires fine-grained contents. But since hearing and thought can have the same content at that level and still be epistemically inequivalent, those contents must be distinct from the modes of presentation that

[73]See Bower and Glass (1976), Palmer (1977), and Winston (1975), all cited in Deutsch and Feroe (1981), p. 520.
[74]Stalnaker (1984), pp. 73–4.

capture epistemic relations. We need all three levels – intension, structure, and mode of presentation – for a satisfactory account.[75]

2.8 Here is where the argument now stands. We have distinguished two kinds of musical hearing, which we have called theory-equivalent and theory-inequivalent. The former is epistemically equivalent to the music-theoretic belief expressed by the content sentence corresponding to an attribution of that hearing; the latter is not. This is to say that theory-inequivalent hearing is nonconceptual in the weak sense, not requiring possession of the music-theoretic concepts used to attribute it.

With respect to content, moreover, the two kinds of hearing differ in the following way: theory-inequivalent hearing and the corresponding theoretical belief have the same intension and the same structure, differing only on the mode of presentation, whereas theory-equivalent hearing has the same content as the corresponding theoretical belief on all three levels. These contrasts provide a more substantive and informative characterization of differences in levels of musical competence – or the distinction between ordinary and expert listeners – than does an appeal to "unconscious" perception or related notions.

But nothing said so far requires us to give up the belief thesis, on which musical hearing is perceptual belief and involves perceptual

---

[75]The reader may have noticed a similarity between my notion of structure and Carnap's notion of *intensional structure* (1956, pp. 56–9). Carnap uses this notion in an attempt to solve the paradox of analysis. On Carnap's view, 'brother' has the same intension as, but a different intensional structure than, 'male sibling'. I cannot undertake a detailed comparison of Carnap's framework and mine here, but I want to point out that I use the notion of structure for more or less the opposite purpose of Carnap's: he uses intensional structure to capture what is different between the two terms, whereas I use the structure to capture what is common between hearing and thought. The epistemic difference between them is, on my view, on another level, that of the mode of presentation.

concepts. We are required at most to say that theory-inequivalent hearing is a matter of having a belief *different* from the corresponding theoretical belief and perceptual concepts distinct from those expressed by the relevant music-theoretic terms. We shall see in the next chapter, however, why we cannot remain content with this view.

3

Musical Hearing as
Strongly Nonconceptual

3.1   In this chapter I shall argue that certain musical hearing is strongly nonconceptual, which is to say that it is not the exercise of any concept (which is stronger than saying it is not the exercise of the music-theoretic concept used to attribute it). In view of the close connection between concepts and belief, this amounts to saying that such hearing is not belief. And since the only kind of belief it could plausibly be is perceptual belief, this amounts to the denial of what I have called the belief thesis (for hearing of the relevant kind).[1]

What precisely must be shown here? Recall that musical hearing is a psychological state named by a hearing ascription (type) such

[1]My notion of 'strongly nonconceptual' resembles, though does not coincide with, one that can be derived from Peacocke: "When we enter a room, even a room full of abstract sculptures, we perceive things in it as having particular shapes: and there is no question of this requiring that we had in advance concepts of these particular shapes" (Peacocke [1986], p. 15, quoted in Crane [1992a], p. 9). The argument to follow owes much to recent discussions of nonconceptual representation and content, but departs from them in its construal of 'nonconceptual'. I cannot undertake an exhaustive comparison here, but shall briefly touch on some of the points of contact, and divergence, in Section 3.5.

57

that a listener is in that state if and only if she satisfies the ascription. The belief thesis says that this psychological state is (*qua* type) a perceptual belief. We want to exhibit some kinds of musical hearing that fail this principle.

3.2 What is it, then, for a given mental state to be a belief?[2] It is (inter alia) for various tokens of that state to involve the same mode of presentation, to be exercises of the same concept. (Recall we stipulated that belief state types are individuated by modes of presentation.) Thus, in order to show that a certain state is not a belief, it is sufficient to show that different tokens of that state are not, as it were, unified under a single concept or mode of presentation in this way.

Suppose, for example, we wanted to show that two perceptual experiences of a color involve different modes of presentation. Call the first mode of presentation of color F, and the second G. It would seem sufficient, in order to demonstrate that F and G are different modes of presentation, to show that one can rationally believe that some object is F, but doubt that it is G.

That is the direct approach, focused, like Frege's famous case, on a single pair of states, one of which is belief, the other doubt. The problem with this approach lies in isolating the *color* as the locus of doubt from the rest of the perceptual presentation. Unless that feature is isolated, it remains open that the cognitive difference to the subject is due to other, irrelevant features of the perceptual situation (and there will always be such). One way to isolate the color is, of course, to use the word 'color' in asking questions of the subject, but in our musical cases the subject typically does not have that sort of linguistic mastery.

So we need to adopt a different strategy, casting our net more widely. It is insufficient to look at a single instance or pair of in-

---

[2]The notion of belief operative here is that of a belief *about* something, e.g., that x is red, so that one may have type-identical beliefs about different objects or events. The relevant notion is, if you will, that of a "one-place" belief.

stances; we must advert rather to general capacities someone will have in virtue of possessing a given perceptual concept or belief. If someone enjoys a certain kind of musical hearing, but does not have the capacities that would be entailed if that hearing were belief, then it cannot be belief.

One such capacity may be derived from the *action-guiding* role of belief, or, more specifically, its connection to discriminative behavior. This role has been stressed by functionalist philosophers of mind, most prominently D. M. Armstrong, whose views I largely follow here.

Functionalism takes mental states to be defined by their causal roles with respect to sensory inputs, behavioral outputs, and other mental states. The causal role of perceptual belief is related to a capacity for selective or discriminative behavior, which consists in treating things of a certain kind, in certain circumstances, "in a systematically different way" from other things.[3] This means treating those things in the same kind of way, but not treating other things in that way. A paradigm case of selective behavior is sorting – for example, sorting red things from non-red things. The perceptual belief that an object is red is a state that is, in an appropriate way, causally responsible for such selective behavior.[4] Having a perceptual concept of red is, in turn, a capacity for having the perceptual belief that a thing is red.[5]

Complications arise from the fact that misperception can occur and that one's discriminative capacities may not be perfect. Fortunately, these complications are not directly relevant for us. What we need is the comparatively weak result that having a certain perceptual belief about each of several objects (or events) entails the capacity to treat *those* objects (i.e., those about which one has the belief) in a

[3]Armstrong (1968), p. 250.

[4]Ibid., p. 210; see also p. 339. The precise way in which the state must enable such behavior is something I will not try to spell out here – not just any enabling would be appropriate – but I suppress this complication.

[5] Ibid., pp. 339–40; see also Armstrong (1973), p. 61.

selective way, regardless of whether one has a capacity to treat selectively the things of which the belief is true.[6] Thus, if one represents objects or events in the same way but has no capacity for selective behavior toward them, then that (type of) representation cannot be a perceptual belief.

A second capacity entailed by the enjoyment of perceptual beliefs and concepts involves the experience and judgment of phenomenal similarity. One is apt to see things about which one has the same perceptual belief *as* the same (in the relevant respect); such things are apt to *look* similar to one in a phenomenologically salient way; one will have a disposition to judge them to be similar. (This aspect of functional role has to do with relations to other mental states, instead of behavioral outputs.) Identity of mode of presentation, then, is a notion that explains recognition: having a perceptual concept of red entails a capacity for recognizing the property from instance to instance, for reidentifying it.[7] Such instances are unified, as it were, under a single concept, or (for us) the mode of presentation that individuates a concept. To have genuine spatial concepts – for example, concepts of particular spatial locations – entails having a framework of stable locations that one can reidentify over time, such that one can meaningfully speak of things being at the same or different places over time.[8] (Concomitant with this are inferential capacities

---

[6]One problem still lurking here, however, is the definition of *behavior*: it is not just any bodily change or response, but connotes purposive activity subject to the will; see Armstrong (1968), pp. 250, 255, 263. Otherwise, the acquisition of radioactivity in one's body (if one is unaware of this) could constitute a discriminative response to radiation.

I have stressed the "efferent," or output, side of the causal role of perceptual beliefs because it is most relevant for us. Concerning the "afferent," or input, side (the terminology is Dennett's [1969], pp. 76–8), some relation of reliable causation, or indication, or covariance of representations with what they represent is surely an important part of the story as well (on indication, see Stalnaker [1984], p. 18; on covariance, Cummins [1989], chs. 4–6).

[7]This idea was prompted in part by Bennett (1966), p. 143.

[8]This stress on reidentification, which I take as a criterion for identity of concept,

such as inferring, when presented with one red object and then another, that at least two things are red.)[9]

Again, if someone mentally represents certain events in the same way but is not disposed to see or hear them as similar, then that (type of) representation cannot be a perceptual belief. Now to show that certain kinds of mental representation of music fail those criteria.

3.3   The kinds of representations I shall discuss are those posited on some models of melody recognition in cognitive psychology. (Such theories, the reader may recall, are intended primarily to describe ordinary rather than expert listeners.)

Now it might seem, at first blush, that any cognitive–psychological theory *must* be about beliefs and concepts (insofar as it is about mental representation, at least). For possession of a certain perceptual belief or concept is (at least on our first criterion) a matter of having a certain discriminative capacity. But what is the central experimental paradigm in cognitive psychology, if not the investigation of a subject's discriminative capacities? It would seem, then, that the kind of mental representations posited in such theories must be perceptual beliefs.[10] However, I shall argue that certain such kinds of representations are not beliefs; they are, rather, what I call strongly nonconceptual representations.

The argument, which is empirical, can be applied to various psychological models (which vary somewhat in importance and sphere of applicability). Here is the schema of the argument. On the given model, a listener (of a certain kind), upon hearing a musical passage (of a certain kind in certain circumstances), will represent certain events in the same way. But the listener has no ability to discriminate

was suggested to me by Strawson (1959), ch. 1. Peacocke (1992b), pp. 90–1, takes a view that is different from mine, on which reidentification is possible at a nonconceptual level.

[9]When perceptual presentations are not simultaneous, at least one corresponding perceptual belief involves memory; it is a perceptual belief about the past.

[10]I took this line in DeBellis (1988).

Example 3.1

between those events and others; nor is he disposed to judge that those events, and only those events, are similar in any salient respect. The said representations of those events are not, in short, unified for that listener under the same concept or mode of presentation. Therefore, that kind of representation cannot (*qua* type) be a perceptual belief.

As a first application, consider the representation of absolute pitch locations.[11] A plausible version of the theory might go like this: as an ordinary listener hears a melody, he has a perceptual representation of the pitch of each note of the melody (a representation that, moreover, is veridical). Thus, in Example 3.1 the listener has a perceptual representation of the first note as f^1 (F above middle C), the next as d^1, and so on. The question is, what sort of mental representation is this?

An ordinary, untrained listener may easily verify by armchair methods that he cannot reliably distinguish instances of f^1 from noninstances; in other words, he cannot sort the pitches of the melody into those that are f^1 and those that are not. This is, moreover, not simply a matter of not knowing what the label 'f^1' refers to; the listener cannot reliably tell, in general, when two pitches of the melody are the same – as on the italicized words in "*Oh*-oh say can you see, by the dawn's early *light*" – and when they are different. He cannot reliably discriminate between same-pitch pairs and different-pitch pairs; he is not (in general) able to grasp them *as* the same. Yet, on the given theory, he has type-identical representations of such pitch-

[11]See Bharucha (1991), pp. 90–1, and Deutsch (1969).

62

es; hence, that representation (*qua* type) cannot be a belief and cannot involve perceptual concepts of absolute pitch locations.

What would it be to have such perceptual concepts? It would simply be to have perfect pitch. Listeners with perfect (absolute) pitch have a stable perceptual framework permitting reliable reidentification of pitch locations over time and selective behavior toward such specific locations.

It is true that in certain limited circumstances it is possible for ordinary listeners to tell when pitches are the same – for example, when they are heard in immediate succession. But this goes at most to show that such listeners have a perceptual concept with a more limited content, namely, a concept of immediately successive same-pitch pairs. One's perceptual concepts are constrained by what one can discriminate; a restricted discrimination ability points at most to a concept with a restricted content. But then that ability is irrelevant to the status of a type of representation that applies to both successive and nonsuccessive pitches.

It may be objected that what I have described is a memory effect. The perceptual representation of a tune, it might be said, consists of beliefs, though very ephemeral ones: by the time the listener hears a later pitch (assuming some appropriate time interval), he has forgotten the location of earlier ones. Then there would be no requirement having to do with phenomenal similarity or recognition, since at no time would the listener have the same belief about different tokens of the same pitch. (There is no requirement that a subject be disposed to infer the consequences of premises he does not hold all at the same time.)

I have three things to say in response to this objection. First, the objection is relevant to the phenomenal-similarity criterion, but not the discriminatory-behavior criterion. It explains why instances of the same pitch do not all sound similar in some salient way to a listener, but not why the listener is unable to behave selectively toward those instances. Second, I do not know whether such a memory limitation is consistent with the purposes of the theories in which such representations are postulated: the theoretical work to be done by those representations may require them to be longer-lived than failure of identity recognition would allow.

Third, the objection is concessive, in a way, because the alleged ephemeral beliefs would function in a much more limited fashion than do, normally, the representations we call conceptual. We ordinarily think of beliefs as fairly stable representations allowing judgments of identity and difference. The ephemeral beliefs envisioned here would function rather differently from beliefs ordinarily conceived; and beyond this the point is largely terminological.

It is of no use to appeal to memory failure, moreover, in the case of representations posited precisely to explain memory for melodies. Let us now apply the argument to such a case. On the relative chroma theory, a listener recognizes a familiar tonal melody (detects errors, etc.) by comparing a perceptual input with a stored representation, where each represents a series of chromas.

What sort of representation is that stored memory trace?[12] Such a representation (of a given chroma) is not a *belief*, because a listener who enjoys that representation need not be able to discriminate between instances of that chroma, or scalestep, and noninstances or to recognize that feature over its instances. How do we know this? By the fact that this is precisely what one learns to do in elementary tonal ear training and that, for most people, this is *work:* it is not a trivial matter of learning to apply labels, but entails the development of new perceptual abilities. This sort of ear training entails the acquisition, or the development, of perceptual concepts of particular scalestep locations – the movable-do system may be especially efficacious for this – and related perceptual concepts, such as that of a perfect fifth (learning to "hear intervals" is a matter of acquiring per-

---

[12]There is an interesting metaphysical issue about what events the stored representations represent: particular past events? fictional events? clusters of events? A memory trace of a familiar tune is ordinarily based on many hearings. But to investigate this would take us too far afield.

ceptual concepts of particular intervals). If ear training did not consist in the development of such concepts, but consisted (say) merely in the association of already-possessed perceptual concepts with verbal labels, then it would be as easy as learning to type – or at any rate it is not clear why it would not be. In contrast to the conceptual representations acquired through this sort of musical training, however, the representations enjoyed by listeners not so trained – that of chroma, for example – are nonconceptual.

It may be objected that what I have described is merely a phenomenon of selective *access*, since we can exploit the stored chroma information only in context, that is, as we are hearing an appropriate segment of the melody.[13] True, but then this stored representation is not a stable, persisting belief since it only intermittently functions as a belief, that is, is available for inference. The larger point is that this failure of access means something about conceptualization. Concepts are general abilities to entertain a given mode of presentation and to recognize and reidentify things under the latter. Selectivity of access points to a fundamental difference in the *kind* of cognition operative here, one significantly different from that involved in conceptualization and belief.

3.4 My point has not, however, been to argue that untrained listeners typically have no musical concepts or no perceptual beliefs in connection with music. The point is rather that one's concepts are constrained by what one can recognize. Most people can recognize "Happy Birthday"; therefore, they have a perceptual concept of "Happy Birthday." They are able to enjoy the perceptual belief that "Happy Birthday" is sounding. The ability to have such a belief – which goes hand in hand with the ability to recognize the tune – may, on prevailing psychological theories, depend on representational capacities such as that of chroma, but the latter capacities are themselves nonconceptual. One's conceptual capacities may depend in this way on nonconceptual ones.

[13]This was suggested to me (not *qua* objection) by Gilbert Harman.

This, I believe, is an important principle, one that clarifies an insight of Gestalt psychology. The Gestaltists' dictum was that the whole is perceptually prior to the parts.[14] Here we see a way in which this is true: there is a certain kind of grasp one has of an entire melody, a conceptual grasp, which does not extend to the individual pitches and intervals that make it up. Only by dint of perceptual training does one develop concepts of such atomic features. At the same time (and this complements the Gestaltist insight) an untrained listener's capacity to recognize a tune does depend on representations of pitches and intervals, but ones that are not conceptual.

Many kinds of mental representations of music are, I submit, nonconceptual. One is the representation of intervals, on the successive-interval model of melody recognition; this may be shown by an argument parallel to those given earlier, and I will not rehearse it here. For another example, let us return to the views of Budd:

It is often not required that someone should recognise something as an instance of a certain concept under which it falls, or even that he should possess the concept, if he is to be aware of that phenomenon in a work of art and understand its role within the work. In the case of music, a listener does not need to have the concept of, say, a dominant seventh chord . . . in order to have a full sensitivity to the harmonic implications of such a chord in a work he is listening to. And, since he does not need to possess the concept, he does not need to bring the chord under the concept when he hears the chord if he is to experience the work with understanding.[15]

Musical understanding entails, then, a sensitivity to the harmonic implications of chords.

The kind of sensitivity to which Budd is referring has, I believe, been explicated by Leonard Meyer. On Meyer's view, a crucial element in musical perception is *expectation:* when we hear a dominant

[14]Wertheimer (1938 [1925]), p. 2; in connection with melody, p. 5.
[15]Budd (1985), p. 246.

chord, for example, we (ordinarily) expect the tonic to follow.[16] As Meyer explains, we assign different subjective probabilities to different possible continuations; our grasp of musical style depends on our possessing "internalized probability systems" in this way.[17] Meyer identifies the latter with "complex systems of subjective probability feelings about musical events. Such internalized, subjective probability systems are the 'beliefs' about which Charles Peirce writes."[18]

The question for us is whether such systems are beliefs in our sense. (I will not inquire into Peirce's.) Suppose when we hear a chord we assign a certain set of subjective probabilities for the chord to follow; call this an expectation matrix. Is having such a matrix a matter of having a *belief* about the chord we are now hearing? If, for example, we hear a dominant chord and we assign a probability of 1 to a tonic continuation, is this a matter of believing the chord we are now hearing to be a certain kind of thing – a "tonic demander," let us say? If so, then it would seem that – if whenever we hear a dominant chord we have a certain kind of expectation matrix – musical understanding is conceptual after all.

But an expectation matrix need not be a belief in our sense. For having a certain expectation matrix is, at bottom, a disposition to be surprised more or less by certain continuations. But being disposed to be surprised by certain continuations in the same way for a given class of events does not entail the ability to discriminate between those events and others. The fact, if it is one, that a listener has a certain type of expectation matrix for all and only dominant chords does not entail that the listener has a capacity for selective, uniform *action* toward all and only dominant chords. Nor does it ensure that dominant chords are the same *for* the listener in any salient way:

---

[16]Meyer (1956) introduces a conception of musical perception and meaning based on expectation that is subsequently developed in later writings. I will not trace that development here.

[17]Ibid., p. 8.

[18]Ibid., p. 261. I owe this reference to Akira Takaoka.

chords that prompt the same expectations need not sound, or be apt to be judged, alike. (The listener does not, after all, know that her expectations are relevantly similar in such cases.)

This point may be extended, I believe, to research on pitch cognition by Carol Krumhansl and others.[19] To cite one experimental paradigm: a subject hears an incomplete musical scale followed by a tone, which in different trials varies in its relation to the scale, and the subject is asked to rate how well the tone completes the pattern.[20] As I understand the results, tokens of the same scale degree tend to be given similar ratings from trial to trial, and certain pairs of scale degrees (e.g., tonic and dominant) tend to be given closer ratings than certain other pairs (e.g., tonic and leading tone). But these results do not show that the subject has perceptual concepts of particular scale degrees.[21] That would require that the subject be able to distinguish instances of a particular scale degree from noninstances; but in the data obtained in Krumhansl's experiment, different scale degrees are sometimes given the same or approximately the same rating,[22] which is consistent with the subject's not being able to discriminate among similarly rated scale degrees.

I hope it is clear that my point is not in any way to challenge or discount the voluminous psychological research on the mental representation of pitch and related parameters. It is rather to put such research in perspective, to say what its significance is. My purpose has been to argue that the kind of mental representation posited by such research is at a different level from conceptual thought, from propositional attitudes such as belief, and to show how and why it is different. But in no way do I claim that there is not some *other* perfectly respectable notion of mental representation on which it may be

[19]Krumhansl (1990); results originally reported in Krumhansl and Shepard (1979).

[20]Krumhansl (1990), p. 21.

[21]Nor does Krumhansl claim that they do.

[22]Krumhansl (1990), p. 23.

supposed that listeners have mental representations of pitch, chroma, and so on.[23] It is just not a notion of representation that entails *recognition* of the properties represented.

We have shown, then, that certain kinds of musical hearing are strongly nonconceptual. The perceptual states posited by certain hearing ascriptions are not, *qua* types, beliefs: their tokens are not unified under a single concept or mode of presentation.

3.5   I want now to briefly compare my notion of "nonconceptual" with related conceptions in the literature. Let me begin with recent discussions whose main purpose is to adumbrate notions of nonconceptual representation or nonconceptual content. Some of these have provided inspiration for the present arguments, but I diverge from them in some ways as well. The writers whose works I shall discuss here are Christopher Peacocke and Tim Crane.[24]

Peacocke has suggested in a number of writings that perception, or experiential content, can be nonconceptual. In one place he suggests that

an experience can have a finer-grained content than can be formulated by using concepts possessed by the experiencer. If you are looking at a range of mountains, it may be correct to say that you see some as rounded, some as jagged. But the content of your visual experience in respect of the shape of the mountains is far more specific than that description indicates.[25]

In another, he writes,

***

[23]That notion will probably depend heavily on the "afferent" side of causal role – involving indication, covariance, etc. For a related discussion, see Dretske (1978), p. 126.

[24]Other writers who have invoked notions of nonconceptual representation or content include, prominently, Gareth Evans; see Evans (1985), p. 377, and (1982), pp. 122–9 and secs. 6.3 and 7.4. For further references to philosophical treatments of these topics, see Crane (1992a) and Peacocke (1986), p. 14n.

[25]Peacocke (1992a), p. 111.

When we enter a room, even a room full of abstract sculptures, we perceive things in it as having particular shapes: and there is no question of this requiring that we had in advance concepts of these particular shapes.[26]

And elsewhere he writes,

The symmetry of an inkblot shape can be perceived by one who does not have the concept of symmetry.[27]

Crane, who provides a helpful gloss on Peacocke's views, has suggested the following definition of the term 'nonconceptual content': "X is in a state with nonconceptual content iff X does not have to possess the concepts that characterise its content in order to be in that state."[28] That definition is more or less in line with what I have been calling *weakly* nonconceptual and seems to be the notion relevant to the third quotation above. The first and second quotations imply a stronger sense of 'nonconceptual', one whereby X may have an experience as of a certain feature without having any concept at all of that feature; that is more or less what I have been calling *strongly* nonconceptual.

The present study complements Peacocke's approach and provides a broader foundation for the tenet that perceptual experience has a nonconceptual dimension. In reading Peacocke – for example, the third quotation above – one is not always sure what the source of the relevant notion of perception is: what the context is in which we attribute such perception to someone and what theoretical role that notion of perception is meant to play. (Why *should* we say that someone who does not have the concept of symmetry can "perceive symmetry"; or, conversely, why we should withhold attributing the, or a, concept of symmetry to someone who satisfies the requirements for

[26]Peacocke (1986), p. 15, quoted in Crane (1992a), p. 9.

[27]Peacocke (1992a), p. 122. (Peacocke goes on to apply the point to musical perception.)

[28]Crane (1992b), p. 149.

attributing the latter?) The present study provides one answer, by turning to actual discourse in music theory and psychology and showing that such discourse induces a notion of nonconceptual representation along Peacocke's lines.

My divergences with Crane are more marked. Crane is concerned to show that perceptual experience has a nonconceptual content (on the earlier definition). The argument depends on two main claims: that "perceptions are not beliefs" – as Crane wants to show from examples like the Müller-Lyer illusion – and that perceptions do not have the inferential structure characteristic of beliefs, namely, conceptual structure.[29]

Perhaps I am missing something, but I do not see how it is more than trivial to say that perception – or indeed any intentional state – has some nonconceptual content or other (on Crane's definition). One level of content is the object perceived (or, by our lights, the corresponding intension), and it is obvious that that object can be characterized using concepts not possessed by the perceiver.[30] That is often the case with referentially transparent ascriptions; and satisfying such an ascription is in no way inconsistent with having a conceptual content at some other level.

I think that in order to understand Crane's claim we must take him to mean 'content' more narrowly: we should understand the claim to be that, at a certain *level* of content (the mode of presentation, perhaps), perceptual experience and conceptual thought have different kinds of content. At the same time, Crane suggests that the content of perceptual experience may be taken to be scenario content (a notion of Peacocke's), which is "a set of ways of filling out the space around the perceiver with properties (colours, shapes, temperatures and so on) relative to an origin and a family of axes."[31] But

---

[29]Ibid., p. 154.

[30]Complications arise when there is no object perceived, e.g., in hallucination, but I shall leave this aside.

[31]Crane (1992b), p. 154, following Peacocke (1992a), pp. 105-7.

scenario content cannot be used to, as it were, *distinguish* perceptual experience from conceptual thought, because the latter too can specify a scenario content. (This is parallel to the way, on the present account, hearing and theoretical belief can specify the same structure.) The notion to invoke in order to drive a wedge between experience and thought might rather be Peacocke's "analogue content."[32]

At any rate, one difference between Crane's approach and mine is that the present approach puts more emphasis on nonconceptual *representation* than on nonconceptual *content:* I have not attempted to argue, as Crane does, for a distinctive kind of content possessed by nonconceptual representations. In my view, it is sufficient to say that different tokens of a nonconceptual representation involve numerically different modes of presentation; it is not necessary to posit different *kinds* of content.

And though elements of the present argument were suggested by Crane's idea that "perceptions are not beliefs," the scope of our claims is different. Crane is arguing that perception *across the board* has a stage that precedes conceptualization.[33] The claim of this chapter is far more limited: it is that *certain features* are nonconceptually represented, not that there is a stage at which all perceived features are.

It would take us too far afield to treat Crane's discussion in detail here, but let me register this doubt: even if his argument that perception is not belief, and that it lacks the inferential structure of beliefs, is successful, I do not see that anything follows about perceptual *contents.* The first point is made via examples such as the Müller-Lyer illusion (the lines that appear to be unequal in length), in which things look a certain way to one, but one does not believe that they are that way.[34] And Crane argues that perceptions do not have the inferential

---

[32]Peacocke (1986).
[33]Crane (1992b), p. 155.
[34]Ibid., p. 150.

structure of beliefs because, though certain deductive and normative relations are constitutive of belief, "there is no such thing as deductive inference *between* perceptions"; moreover, "to perceive that *p*, there are no other *perceptions* that you *ought to* have. There is no 'ought' about it."[35] And though it is a constraint on belief that "we cannot have explicitly contradictory conscious beliefs," the Waterfall Illusion, in which things appear to be both moving and not moving, is an instance of "a conscious perception with an explicitly contradictory content."[36] Even if all of this is true, I do not see how it follows that perception and belief have different kinds of content, or even that perceiving that *p* has a numerically different content from believing that *p*, as opposed to being different *attitudes* toward the *same* content. Indeed, if Crane's argument were sound, it could be marshaled to show that all propositional attitudes – ones with the same conceptual contents as belief – must exhibit the inferential structure of the latter. But surely that is not so. Consider *entertaining the thought that p*, for example: the constraints that must be satisfied in order for it to be the thought that *p* that you are entertaining are going to be different from those that must be satisfied in the case of belief. But it does not follow from this that entertaining the thought that *p*, and believing that *p*, have different contents.[37]

To return briefly to Peacocke, I want to note a particular argument of his – which Crane calls "one route to the thesis that perceptions have nonconceptual contents" – simply in order to say that that argument is rather different from the present one, and therefore

---

[35]Ibid., pp. 152, 154.

[36]Ibid., p. 152. See also Crane (1988).

[37]It is unclear, moreover, what is shown by the fact that a certain class of states does not exhibit properties possessed by the class of beliefs as a whole. The class of beliefs one acquires on Tuesdays might not exhibit the same structure as the class of beliefs generally, but so what? And even if Crane is right that we do not infer perceptions directly from other perceptions, there is much to recommend the view that perception does depend on inference and is part of one's total belief system; see Bruner (1957) and Harman (1973), ch. 11.

what it establishes may well be different from anything shown here.[38] Peacocke's argument goes like this: two lines may appear to you to have the same length, though you suspect (without doubting your senses) that they are not precisely the same length; it follows then that the "manner" of perception, on which they appear to have the same length, is distinct from the "demonstrative mode of presentation," on which you think of them as possibly having different lengths.[39]

It is not clear to me, however, why the argument should be taken to demonstrate the existence of a distinctively nonconceptual *kind* of content, as opposed to understanding the case as one in which numerically different modes of presentation are involved in perceptual belief and nonperceptual thought. (Moreover, it seems plausible to say that different properties are being presented in perception and thought: lengths to one degree of exactitude in the case of thought, to a lesser degree in the case of perception.) At any rate, the present argument for nonconceptuality is not as subtle as this. Peacocke's argument trades on the idea that things may be phenomenally similar to one, but that one may still doubt whether they are the same; the conclusion, then, is that the level at which they are phenomenally similar is nonconceptual. But for the kinds of musical perception discussed in the present chapter, not even phenomenal similarity obtains. The kind of nonconceptuality I am arguing for is more at the level of Peacocke's manners of perception than at the level of his demonstrative modes of presentation; I do not make the further move, as Peacocke does, of driving a wedge between the two.

3.6 I want to briefly consider once more the relevance of the notion of unconscious perception to musical hearing. I argued earlier that weak nonconceptuality – informational inequivalence between

---

[38]Crane (1992a), p. 10; the argument about to be discussed is that in Peacocke (1989), pp. 306–8.

[39]Peacocke (1989), pp. 306–8.

hearing and thought, which is concomitant with lack of verbal re-portability – is no reason to say hearing is unconscious. Does strong nonconceptuality alter the picture?

I do not think it does. The fact that someone does not *recognize* the same thing or property from one occasion to the next does not mean that he is not *conscious* of that thing or property on either occasion; we do not say that someone who thinks of Venus on one occasion as the Evening Star and on another as the Morning Star (not appreci-ating the identity) must thereby be representing Venus unconscious-ly. Likewise, then, for chroma representation: the fact that listeners cannot reidentify chroma properties does not mean they do not con-sciously experience them. If such representations of music are in-deed both conscious and nonconceptual, then they are an instance precisely of what Peacocke and Crane are arguing for: the possession of a nonconceptual dimension by perceptual *experience*.

What is the relation of the notion of strongly nonconceptual rep-resentation to Stich's notion of subdoxastic states? Recall that the two main attributes of subdoxastic states are that they are uncon-scious and that they lack inferential integration. Having just consid-ered the first, let me turn to the second. Strongly nonconceptual hearing exhibits lack of inferential integration in, among other ways, the following: for a given state of hearing (*qua* type), tokens of that type are not inferentially integrated with one another; for example, the representation of each of two sound-events x and y as $\hat{3}$ (and the belief that x is distinct from y) need not lead to the conclusion that at least two sound-events are $\hat{3}$. (This is in contrast to the kind of inte-gration failure we noted in the preceding chapter, where hearing is unintegrated with theoretical belief.)

Thus, the present notion of strongly nonconceptual hearing is akin to Stich's notion of subdoxastic state, at least with respect to the constraint of inferential integration.

3.7 To recapitulate the argument up to this point. In the preced-ing chapter I argued that there is a kind of musical hearing that is weakly nonconceptual, which is to say that it is theory-inequivalent: someone can be in that state without having the music-theoretic concepts used to attribute it; and that is one difference between the ordinary listener's hearing and the trained listener's, for the latter, I have maintained, is characteristically theory-equivalent. In this chapter I have argued that certain musical hearing is, moreover, strongly nonconceptual, which is to say that it is not identical with any perceptual belief: its tokens are not unified by a single concept or mode of presentation. This is a second respect in which an ordinary listener's hearing contrasts with that of a trained listener.

But I shall end this chapter with a puzzle. The puzzle arises from the fact that a music analyst is often able to *recognize* an analysis as true to her hearing (before reading or undertaking the analysis), while at the same time it seems that she *learns* or *discovers* something about that hearing through the analysis. The analyst is the authority for the correctness of the analysis *qua* description of her hearing, at the same time that the analysis apparently reveals something to her about that hearing. The question is whether, and how, both of these can be true at once.

Consider, for example, GTTM's grouping analysis of the opening of Beethoven's Piano Sonata op. 2, no. 2 (Example 3.2).[40] Our response to this analysis is likely to have two components. First, we recognize – the intuition is quite strong – that the analysis is true to the way we have heard the passage, prior to encountering the analysis.[41] Second, we feel we have learned something, either about the piece or about how we have been hearing it, from the analysis.

The assumption of epistemic equivalence of analysis and hearing that I have made explains the recognition: it accounts for (in a way that shows to be justified) the intuition that the analysis correctly describes our hearing. But it leaves quite unintelligible the element of

[40]Lerdahl and Jackendoff (1983), p. 15.

[41]The stipulation is important because otherwise the informativeness of the analysis is not quite so problematic. Sometimes, of course, a musical analysis causes us to hear a piece in a new way – but not always.

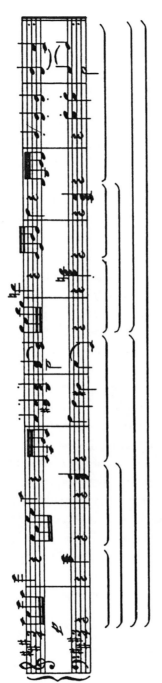

Example 3.2

discovery, of why musical analyses have any interest for us whose hearing they describe, why they seem to be sources of learning or discovery for us. For if they contain no more information than do those perceptual states, they will not tell us anything we did not already know; they will be uninformative to us, like statements of our ordinary beliefs. The statement, for example, that Bill Clinton is a Democrat is something I recognize as a statement of one of my beliefs, but (just for this reason) it is not exactly a source of much interest or revelation to me. Musical analyses that we recognize as true to our hearing are precisely *not* trivial or uninteresting in this way (much of the time); but then they must, in their information content, go beyond the hearings they describe.[42] Positing epistemic equivalence of hearing and analysis explains, then, the *authority* an expert listener has in identifying the analyses that are true to his hearing, but not the *interest* those analyses have for him. The problem is analogous to the paradox of analysis: if analytic equivalence – e.g., between 'brother' and 'male sibling' – is identified with epistemic equivalence, it follows that true statements of analytic equivalence must be trivial. As Carnap points out, once we draw the proper distinction between those levels of meaning, the paradox dissolves.[43]

If the foregoing is correct, then, even for an expert listener, hearing and analysis are not epistemically equivalent (and this, unfortunately, will spoil – or at least complicate – the neat picture we had of the contrast between ordinary and expert listeners). But rather than cry over (possibly) spilled milk, I want to point to one further question that arises. If – as must then be the case – the analyst's recognition of an analysis as true to his hearing is a matter of inference, what sort of knowledge lies behind that inference? What sort of knowledge is it that justifies the analyst's "intuition" that *this*, rather

---

[42]It might be argued that the new information is second-order: that one comes to be aware *that* one hears a passage as such-and-such. I find this intuitively unpersuasive.

[43]Carnap (1956), p. 64. On the paradox of analysis, see Moore (1942), pp. 660–7, cited by Carnap (1956), p. 63, and other references cited in the latter.

than that, analysis corresponds to his hearing? I doubt that it is a posteriori, since there is no experience the effect of which is to learn that certain analyses match up with certain hearings. The relevant knowledge is, I suspect, something like our knowledge of analytic (not epistemic) equivalences, such as that between 'brother' and 'male sibling'; thus, the hoary issues of analyticity manage to insinuate their way even into musical analysis. But at this point I have not worked out my view of the matter beyond this, and so shall let it rest here.

In the next two chapters I want to take up some of the cognitive and aesthetic implications of the sort of hearing informed by theory. (I will continue to call it "theory-laden," without prejudice to the question of epistemic equivalence.)

4

Is There an Observation–Theory
Distinction in Music?

4.1   In a now-classic discussion of the role of observation in science, Norwood Russell Hanson asked us to imagine Tycho Brahe and Johannes Kepler standing on a hill, watching the sunrise. Tycho believed that the sun moved around a fixed earth; Kepler held a heliocentric conception. Hanson wanted to know: "Do Kepler and Tycho see the same thing in the east at dawn?"[1]

Hanson argued that there is an important sense of 'see' in which Kepler and Tycho may well see different things. It would be a mistake, according to Hanson, to assume that Kepler and Tycho must have exactly the same visual data and differ at most in the interpretations they place on them. "Seeing is a 'theory-laden' undertaking," Hanson urged.[2] Kepler and Tycho are apt to make different observations corresponding to their different theoretical commitments: one sees the descent of the horizon with respect to the sun, the other the sun's rising above the horizon.[3] In much the same way, the physicist sees an X-ray tube, the child "a complicated lamp bulb"; one

[1]Hanson (1958), p. 5, italics omitted.
[2]Ibid., p. 19.
[3]Ibid., p. 182n.

microbiologist sees a Golgi body, another a cluster of staining material.[4]

One writer who has drawn out the implications of this conception of observation is Thomas Kuhn. Like Hanson, Kuhn believed that scientific disagreement is not simply a matter of coming to different interpretations of the same "individual and stable data."[5] There is often no theory-neutral, Archimedean standpoint from which to adjudicate scientific disputes, Kuhn maintained: competing scientific theories are often "incommensurable," and when one theory supplants another, a scientist "see[s] a new gestalt" and "respond[s] to a different world."[6] In response, Kuhn's critics have charged him with portraying theory change as irrational, or at least with failing to provide an adequate account of what is rational in it.[7]

These issues arise with full force for – and go to the heart of our understanding of – musical perception and theory. Hanson himself points out the relevance of music to his claims: "The interpretation of a piece of music is there in the music. Where else could it be? It is not something superimposed on pure, unadulterated sound."[8] But does it follow that no distinction is possible between what we hear and what we think about what we hear? If we interpret a piece in a certain way, does it automatically follow that we can *hear* it in that way? Can we (with suitable training) hear any music-theoretic structure we like? And if it is meaningful to speak of rationality in connection with the evaluation and acceptance of theories of music, what role, if any, does observation play in accounting for what is rational in them?

In this chapter, I shall approach these issues by way of an exchange between Paul Churchland and Jerry Fodor. Churchland has

[4]Ibid., pp. 17, 4.

[5]Kuhn (1970), p. 121; citation to Hanson (1958), p. 113.

[6]Kuhn (1970), pp. 111–12.

[7]See, e.g., Shapere (1966) and essays by Karl Popper and Imre Lakatos in Lakatos and Musgrave (1970), all cited in Kuhn (1970), p. 186.

[8]Hanson (1958), p. 23; see also p. 17.

for some time maintained a version of the claim that observation is theory-laden, arguing that perception is highly plastic in response to the theories one holds. Seeking to resist the irrationalism that allegedly follows from such a picture, Fodor has put forth a conception of observation, drawn from modularity theory, for which he claims theory neutrality. Their exchange is particularly relevant in that Churchland holds up trained musical perception as a clear and important example of plasticity, whereas Fodor denies that it is.

The main question I shall address in this chapter is whether trained musical perception – of more or less the kind Churchland invokes – is both theory-laden and observational in Fodor's sense, and hence a counterexample to his view. Much of the task will consist in spelling out just what it is for something to be observational in his sense. A second question, which I shall take up toward the end of the chapter, is whether the example of trained musical perception should lead to worries about relativism or irrationality in theory choice. My agenda, therefore, is twofold: to examine the implications of musical perception for a theory of mental organization, on the one hand, and for epistemology, on the other.

Modularity theory, and allied issues about the relation between perception and cognition, are of much interest in current music theory and music psychology.[9] As we shall see, Fodor puts much weight on a distinction akin to that between perception and cognition, and insists that trained musical perception falls on the latter side of the divide. My goal is to show what is at stake in locating a given kind of mental activity on one side or the other of such a dichotomy, and hence what a debate over whether musical hearing is perception or cognition is a disagreement *about*. With this goal in mind, I shall begin by recounting the exchange between Fodor and Churchland in general terms. I will then turn to the specific case of musical hearing

[9]See, e.g., Narmour (1990), p. 4; Camilleri (1989); Jackendoff (1987), pp. 247–72; and Jackendoff (1991), p. 221. For a helpful overview and discussion of the role of modularity in several music theories, see Cumming (1993).

in an attempt to get to the bottom of the disagreement, and to resolve it.

4.2   Churchland gives the plasticity thesis a full, spirited exposition and defense in *Scientific Realism and the Plasticity of Mind* (hereafter, *SRPM*).[10] He begins from the premise that "perception consists in the conceptual exploitation of the natural information contained in our sensations or sensory states" (*SRPM*, p. 7). The plasticity thesis is the claim that the terms in which one perceives the world are highly dependent on one's conceptual framework or theory. Churchland imagines what it would be like if our perceptual states were laden with a comprehensive scientific theory. People so endowed, he explains,

do not sit on the beach and listen to the steady roar of the pounding surf. They sit on the beach and listen to the aperiodic atmospheric compression waves produced as the coherent energy of the ocean waves is audibly redistributed in the chaotic turbulence of the shallows. . . . They do not observe the western sky redden as the Sun sets. They observe the wavelength distribution of incoming solar radiation shift towards the longer wavelengths (about 0.7×10^{-6} m) as the shorter are increasingly scattered away from the lengthening atmospheric path they must take as terrestrial rotation turns us slowly away from their source.[11]

It is important to see that, on Churchland's view, perception is not the same as sensation, but is the "conceptual exploitation" of sensation. Since perception involves the use or application of concepts, perceptual states have a semantic content: they are *about* something, namely, things or states of affairs in the world to which those concepts apply.

Churchland holds, not surprisingly, that perceptual plasticity has important implications for epistemology. Plasticity illustrates that, as he writes in a later article, "observational knowledge always and in-

[10]Churchland (1979).
[11]*SRPM*, p. 29, quoted in Fodor (1984).

evitably involves some theoretical presuppositions or prejudicial processing."[12] Because observation is theory-laden, Churchland believes, the traditional foundationalist account of our "epistemic adventure" – which asserts that theoretical knowledge rests on epistemically privileged, theory-neutral data – cannot be maintained. We must turn instead to "a more global story of the nature of theoretical justification and rational belief" (e.g., a coherentist account).[13]

In arguing for perceptual plasticity's existence and epistemological import, Churchland is expressing a view along much the same lines as that of Hanson and Kuhn and shared in broad terms by many other philosophers. One of them, Nelson Goodman, states the position vividly:

There is no innocent eye. . . . Not only how but what it sees is regulated by need and prejudice. It selects, rejects, organizes, discriminates, associates, classifies, analyzes, constructs. It does not so much mirror as take and make; and what it takes and makes it sees not bare . . . but as things, as food, as people, as enemies, as stars, as weapons.[14]

Goodman has claimed empirical support, in turn, from the "New Look" psychology of Jerome Bruner and others, which emphasizes the dependence of perceptual processes on beliefs and values.[15]

Claims for the existence of perceptual plasticity can, in fact, be traced at least as far back as Locke. According to Locke:

The *Ideas we receive by sensation, are often* in grown People *alter'd by the Judgment,* without our taking notice of it. When we set before our Eyes a round Globe, of any uniform colour . . .'tis certain, that the *Idea* thereby imprinted in our Mind, is of a flat Circle variously shadow'd. . . . But we

---

[12]Churchland (1988), p. 167.

[13]On foundationalism and coherentism, see Chisholm (1977), p. 63.

[14]Goodman (1976), pp. 7–8. Connections to Hanson, Kuhn, Goodman, and (as I am about to make) Bruner are all drawn by Fodor (1984), pp. 241–3, to whose exposition I am indebted.

[15]Bruner (1957), cited in Goodman (1976), p. 7.

having by use been accustomed to perceive, what kind of appearance convex Bodies are wont to make in us . . . the Judgment . . . alters the Appearances into their Causes . . . and frames to it self the perception of a convex Figure, and an uniform Colour; when the *Idea* we receive from thence, is only a Plain variously colour'd, as is evident in Painting.[16]

It is clear from this passage that Locke thinks of perceptual appearances as laden in some way with concepts and knowledge.

In "Observation Reconsidered" (hereafter, "OR"), Fodor seeks to counter the plasticity view by isolating a kind of observation that will qualify as theory-neutral. Fodor sees this as important because

part of the story about scientific consensus turns crucially on the theory neutrality of observation. Because the way one sees the world is largely independent of one's theoretical attachments, it is possible to see that the predictions – even of theories that one likes a lot – aren't coming out. . . . [I]t is often possible for scientists whose theoretical attachments differ to agree on what experiments would be relevant to deciding between their views, and to agree on how to describe the outcomes of the experiments once they've been run. . . .

The thing is: if you don't think that theory-neutral observation can settle scientific disputes, you're likely to think that they are settled by appeals to coherence, or convention or – worse yet – by mere consensus. And . . . a Realist . . . doesn't see how any of those could compel *rational* belief. ("OR," pp. 250–1)

Fodor draws his notion of observation from the conception of the mind set forth in *The Modularity of Mind* (hereafter, *MM*).[17] Fodor's modularity theory is a computationalist one, on which mental processes are thought of as computational processes on mental representations (*MM*, p. 39). In Fodor's theory, the mind contains distinct kinds of systems: central systems and input systems, where the latter, in turn, consist of "the perceptual systems plus language" (*MM*, p. 44, italics omitted). It is the function of perceptual systems

[16]Locke (1975 [1700]), II.ix.8, p. 145.
[17]"OR," pp. 245–6, citing Fodor (1983).

"to so represent the world as to make it accessible to thought" (*MM*, p. 40).[18] The central idea of modularity psychology is that input systems – and hence perceptual systems – are modules (*MM*, p. 46). This means that input systems have "most or all" of a certain cluster of properties: domain specificity, fast and mandatory operation, limited central access, fixed neural architecture, characteristic breakdown patterns, characteristic ontogenic development, "shallow" outputs, and informational encapsulation (*MM*, pp. 47–101 passim). The last two features are most relevant for us; we shall consider encapsulation here and return to the level of outputs later.

That input systems are encapsulated means that their mechanisms of information processing are isolated from the background beliefs, goals, desires, and so on, of the subject (*MM*, p. 64). As an example of encapsulation, Fodor cites the Müller-Lyer illusion. The lines look different in length, although we believe that they are the same length:

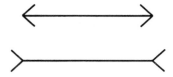

Fodor takes this to illustrate the way in which computations in the visual system are insensitive to background beliefs (*MM*, p. 66; "OR," p. 242).

Unlike input systems, central systems are general purpose in nature, serving thought about a variety of domains (*MM*, pp. 101–3). Central systems include mechanisms of belief fixation: it is in such systems that beliefs are arrived at (*MM*, p. 102). The most important contrast between central systems and input systems is in respect of encapsulation. In central systems, beliefs are revised in a more or less holistic fashion: holding a particular belief may depend on having

[18]In a way this quotation expresses the essence of Fodor's idea of perception, and I am indebted to Cumming (1993), p. 42, for pointing out its centrality.

background beliefs that are (intuitively speaking) quite remote from, or only indirectly connected to, the given belief. For example, your belief about whether it is really Jones you see coming out of the train station will depend on your views about whether Jones could have traveled here by train, whether the trains are running, and so on.

Fodor asserts a distinction between the "fixation of perceptual belief" and the operation of a perceptual system per se (*MM*, p. 136n). The former is a task for central systems and consists in evaluating the output of a perceptual system "in light of background information" (*MM*, p. 46). What it is to be a perceptual belief arrived at in this way should not be conflated with what it is to be the output of the perceptual system proper, which is a *hypothesis* (*MM*, p. 136n). A hypothesis that is the output of a perceptual system – which I shall call a *perceptual hypothesis*, though Fodor nowhere uses this very term – may or may not, on Fodor's view, survive the process of belief fixation and come to serve as a belief.[19] In pointing to the distinction between perceptual beliefs and perceptual hypotheses, Fodor in effect acknowledges, as by rights he must, that not *all* mental processes that begin with sensory stimulation are encapsulated; his contention is simply that the production of perceptual hypotheses is encapsulated. It is these hypotheses that he enlists to play the role of theory-neutral observations ("OR," p. 248).[20]

In calling the output of a perceptual system a "hypothesis," Fodor

---

[19] What I am speaking of here is the content of the relevant representation, not the representation itself: I want to leave it open whether we should think of perceptual belief and perceptual hypothesis as distinct representations, or think of a perceptual belief as a certain kind of representation, namely, a perceptual hypothesis that functions as a belief. As far as I can see, Fodor himself leaves this open. The latter idea is derived from Harman (1973), p. 182.

Though Fodor speaks of hypotheses rather than perceptual hypotheses, the latter term distinguishes the relevant kind from hypotheses in general and is less cumbersome than "output of a perceptual system."

[20] Note that Fodor does not simply identify observation with perception, but rather seeks to explicate one useful notion of observation in terms of perception.

implies that it has a semantic content: it is about features of, or states of affairs in, the world (*MM*, p. 136n).[21] Since such outputs have semantic values, it is meaningful to speak, as Fodor does, of "the vocabulary in which [perceptual] hypotheses are couched" (*MM*, p. 136n). Fodor and Churchland are thus agreed on what perception is in one fundamental respect: it has a semantic content having to do with the world external to the perceiver.[22]

A point of clarification about the meaning of the term 'perceptual belief'. One might think – given the way the distinction between perceptual hypotheses and perceptual beliefs has been drawn – that Fodor takes the class of perceptual beliefs to consist *only* of the perceptual hypotheses that survive belief revision. But I take it that Fodor also understands perceptual beliefs to include products of subsequent inference from such hypotheses ("subsequent," because perceptual processes are themselves inferential ["OR," p. 244]). Fodor remarks that the output of modules is in a "restricted conceptual repertoire," whereas perceptual belief fixation is performed "in light of the totality of background theory" ("OR," p. 249). This suggests that the "conceptual repertoire" of perceptual beliefs is wider than that of perceptual hypotheses, from which it follows that perceptual beliefs are not merely a subset of perceptual hypotheses. (Although it is convenient to decide this essentially terminological issue in this way, nothing crucial hinges on it; points I shall make later in terms of perceptual belief might be recast without reference to that notion.)

Fodor distinguishes between encapsulation on different time scales, synchronic and diachronic ("OR," pp. 247–8). Synchronic encapsulation is a matter of the short term, diachronic the long

[21]Elsewhere, Fodor calls the output of a perceptual module a "judgment" (albeit one correctable by higher cognition), again implying that it has a semantic content. See Fodor's (1988) "Reply to Churchland's 'Perceptual Plasticity and Theoretical Neutrality,'" reprinted in Fodor (1990) (hereafter, "Reply").

[22]Like Churchland, Fodor distinguishes perception from lower-level processes more aptly termed 'sensation': this is the level of the transducer (*MM*, p. 41). In contrast with Churchland, however, Fodor assigns a semantic value to this level also.

term. An example of synchronic encapsulation is someone putting on inverting spectacles, and things looking upside down to her even though she believes they are right side up. But suppose that as she continues to wear the lenses things eventually come to look right side up, and that their looking this way comes about in part because of her beliefs about how they are. That would be a failure of *diachronic* encapsulation. A failure of diachronic encapsulation is a change, over time, of how things look to a person in a way informationally sensitive to the beliefs she holds. (It is commonly said that things come to look right side up to a wearer of inverting spectacles, although Fodor disputes whether this depends on the perceiver's beliefs in a way that would mean failure of encapsulation ["Reply," pp. 258–9].)[23] Clearly, synchronic encapsulation does not entail diachronic encapsulation: for the wearer of inverting lenses, visual perception might at any given time be automatic and insusceptible to present influence by background belief, though over the longer time span adaptation occurs.

We are now in a position to see how the debate over plasticity and theory neutrality can be formulated in Fodor's terms. The issue is one of the "vocabulary in which [perceptual] hypotheses are couched." Is that vocabulary radically malleable in response to the theories we hold? If it is, then we have a certain kind of failure of diachronic encapsulation: the terms in which one perceives the world are changed by the theory to which one subscribes.[24] That is, in essence, the plasticity thesis (stated in Fodor's terms; I do not say that Churchland would accept all of the presuppositions of this formula-

---

[23]See also Churchland (1988), pp. 174–5. For studies of inverting lenses, see Dolezal (1982). Diverging from the usual story, Dolezal insists that adaptation to the lenses does not result in experiences indistinguishable from those before adopting the spectacles (p. 228).

[24]Churchland (1988), pp. 176–7. As I shall explain later, the issues of theory neutrality and diachronic encapsulation do not coincide exactly; but Fodor and Churchland both cast the debate in terms of diachronic encapsulation, and I shall follow their exposition.

tion). If, on the other hand, the perceptual vocabulary is substantially fixed or restricted, then Fodor has, in the perceptual hypothesis, a viable candidate for the role of theory-neutral observation.

Plasticity is, on this construal, one kind of (supposed) failure of diachronic encapsulation. It is this kind of encapsulation on which, most crucially, Fodor's conception of theory-neutral observation depends; for one cannot appeal to perceptual hypotheses for a neutral observation language if their vocabulary is theory-dependent.

4.3   I want to turn now to the main phenomenon of interest, trained musical perception. Although Churchland's discussion of the example is brief, he clearly takes it to be important. It is worth quoting him at length:

Consider the conceptual framework used for describing pitch in musical theory. . . . [T]he chromatic scale and its various properties form the foundation of musical theory. Clearly, however, this conceptual framework is not innate to our auditory processing, nor is it part of ordinary language. But people are regularly trained to use it in auditory perception. . . .

More intricately yet, there is the domain of musical chords, and of harmonious sequences of chords. . . . These also can be directly recognized, by ear, by one suitably practiced in the relevant theory and vocabulary. Such a person perceives, in any composition whether great or mundane, a structure, development, and rationale that is lost on the untrained ear.

We are contemplating a musical example not because it is the only empirical example one can cite, but because it is an unproblematic example. Everyone knows that the 'ear' can be 'trained', as we say, to sustain these remarkable and nonstandard perceptual capabilities. But the example of trained musical perception is a straightforward existence proof for the possibility of theoretically-transformed perception in general.[25]

A couple of remarks are in order. First, we need not be distracted

[25]Ibid., p. 179.

by reservations we might have concerning Churchland's ideas about what is foundational in music theory or what is important in aural training. His point is that musicians receive a certain perceptual training that brings with it a certain theoretical framework, and that is, I think, unexceptionable. There is fairly common agreement on what aural training in music amounts to, at least at an elementary level: it confers the ability, for example, to distinguish major from minor triads, to identify intervals, and to label the pitches of a tonal melody according to scale degree. By "trained musical perception" I mean perception that results from training of this elementary sort, and my purpose is to ask whether this sort of elementary, trained musical perception supports Churchland's contention. (Parallel questions may be asked about the effects of other kinds or levels of musical training, but that is not the present project.)

Second, it should be stressed that the example pertains to the *trained* listener. Much recent work in music theory and cognitive psychology has been concerned with the cognitive capacities of untrained listeners, and it is independently interesting to ask what light is shed by such capacities on the issues of plasticity and theory neutrality. But the present example is a different one, having to do with certain *extra*ordinary perceptual abilities, namely, discriminations and identifications of the sort one typically learns to make in elementary ear training, in a context that is explicitly theoretical.

Fodor has this to say about Churchland's example of musical perception:

This merely begs the question, which is whether the effects of musical training are, in fact, perceptual. Churchland adds that one can "just as easily learn to recognize sounds under their dominant *frequency* description,". . . but again no argument is provided that someone who has learned this has learned to perceive differently (as opposed to having learned a different way of labelling his perceptions and a different theory about what his perceptions are perceptions *of* . . .).

What Churchland has to show is, first, that *perceptual* capacities are altered by learning musical theory (as opposed to the truism that learning musical theory alters what you know about music); second, that it's learning the theory (as opposed to just listening to lots of music) that alters the perception; and third, that perception is altered in some different way if you learn not musical theory but acoustics . . . . [Y]ou don't refuse modularity theory by the unsupported assertion that it is contrary to the facts. ("Reply," p. 260)

At this point the reader may be experiencing vertigo. What is hard to get a grip on here is just what is at issue and who has the burden of proof. To put it in terms of a concrete example: suppose that, as a result of musical training, you hear a given pitch as a dominant. Churchland will say this is an instance of perceptual plasticity; Fodor, on the other hand, will argue that Churchland begs the question by assuming that the relevant mental state is *perceptual,* which on Fodor's view it is not. But what exactly does Fodor think Churchland has to establish in order to show that the given state is *perceptual?* And if it is not clear what has to be established (as I think it is not), who has the burden of spelling it out, Churchland or Fodor?[26]

An interesting twist to the argument is provided by the fact that there is an asymmetry between Churchland's and Fodor's positions.

---

[26]I take it that, of the three questions Fodor raises, it is the first – whether "*perceptual* capacities are altered by learning musical theory" – that is fundamentally at issue. As to the second – whether "it's learning the theory (as opposed to just listening to lots of music) that alters the perception" – I think it is plausible to respond that, typically, knowledge of music theory does, as a matter of psychological fact, enter essentially into ear training. Perhaps it is possible to acquire the relevant discriminative capacities by another route, one that does not involve explicit knowledge of theory, but I do not see why such perceptual learning would be any more palatable to Fodor, given his epistemological aim (namely, delimiting a theory-neutral observation language). There would still be a change of perceptual vocabulary, and the relevant perceptual hypotheses would still be theory-laden, though the theory would be tacit for those perceivers. We shall return to this point later.

To forestall a possible confusion: Fodor is *not* saying that Churchland has to show that simply learning music theory is enough to give someone a trained ear. I think it is agreed on all hands that, on the plasticity thesis, practice in making observations may be required as well (but see Churchland [1988], p. 175).

In order to argue for theory neutrality, Fodor is concerned to draw a distinction between cognitive states that arise from sensory stimulation: those that are *echt* perceptual and those that are not. Churchland does not need to draw any such distinction.[27]

To get a grip on the issue, we must recognize that Fodor's ultimate goal is to show that Churchland's argument poses no threat to his conception of theory neutrality. Since that conception is based on modularity theory, the interesting and relevant question then becomes whether by Fodor's own lights the musical case is perceptual. In terms of our example: is your hearing the pitch as a dominant a perceptual hypothesis or a perceptual belief resulting from subsequent inference? If the former, then (at least prima facie) we have a change of perceptual vocabulary, a failure of diachronic encapsulation, and an instance of a theory-laden perceptual hypothesis; if the latter, not. Perhaps Churchland has, for his part, begged the question by failing to demonstrate that trained musical perception is a perceptual hypothesis in Fodor's sense; but surely there is a fact of the matter about this, one we might well explore.

Our main task, then, is to determine whether trained musical perception is perceptual in Fodor's sense. If it is, then it is a (prima facie) counterexample to the thesis that perception, in his sense, is diachronically encapsulated and to the thesis that perception, in his sense, is theory-neutral. And refutation of the latter would spell doom for Fodor's epistemological aims.

Let me say that in formulating the task in this way, I am taking Fodor's own response to the example as a cue. It is clear that Fodor takes the example to purport to be an instance of unencapsulated perception; he responds by saying it is not such an instance or that it

---

[27]That is the common wisdom ("OR," p. 238), although I am not altogether sure it is correct. Perhaps, ultimately, appreciating the full force and value of the plasticity thesis – or Hanson's insight that Kepler and Tycho may *see* different things – does require one to make a serious distinction between the perceptual and the nonperceptual. But, as I shall explain, I do not think it is obligatory to predicate this distinction on theory neutrality (cf. "OR," p. 237).

has not been shown to be. A different response would be to grant that it is such an instance, but to contend that this holds no peril for theory neutrality. This different way of responding is, I think, open to Fodor. He writes at one point, "The epistemologically relevant question is not whether modules are perfectly encapsulated, but whether they are encapsulated enough to permit theory-neutral, observational resolution of scientific disputes" ("Reply," p. 255). This suggests a different way of responding to the example of trained musical perception: to admit failure of encapsulation, but not of a sort that would be worrisome for the rationality of theory choice. Later I will consider a version of this alternative response. But it is not Fodor's actual response, at any rate; he accepts the worry about encapsulation as real, and I shall follow his lead in this.

One last remark before proceeding. In current discourse about music and modularity, not much weight has been placed on the distinction between synchronic and diachronic encapsulation, if indeed it has been recognized at all. Eugene Narmour, for example, stipulates that the "bottom-up" system in his theory is both "innate" and "automatic."[28] But there is no need to insist that what is automatic must be innate – that is, that what is synchronically encapsulated must be diachronically so. These questions should be separated more than they have been. Diachronic encapsulation – in particular the malleability of the perceptual output vocabulary – is far more interesting than synchronic, because it has the greater implications for epistemology.

4.4   Let us turn now to the task of seeing whether music perception provides an example of a theory-laden perceptual hypothesis, and hence a counterexample to Fodor. The question is whether perceptual training in music brings about a change in the "vocabulary" of perceptual hypotheses – that is, whether one's perceptual system comes to generate hypotheses in music-theoretic terms.

[28]Narmour (1990), p. 55.

At this juncture, the distinction between perceptual hypotheses and perceptual beliefs that are the product of subsequent inference is crucial. It is not at issue whether a trained listener comes to have *beliefs* at some level or other about the sounding of minor or major triads, perfect fifths, and so on, in the course of hearing music; that is granted. The question is whether the *hypotheses* themselves, the output of perceptual systems, are couched in that vocabulary.

The decisive issue is how, on modularity theory, the boundaries of a perceptual system are drawn. In particular, what, if anything, determines where a perceptual system ends – and therefore what its output is – and where what counts as being outside of it begins?

One possible answer would be that the diachronic-encapsulation condition itself largely determines that boundary. It would follow that musically trained hearing is not perceptual in the relevant sense simply because there is a failure of diachronic encapsulation. This would motivate a response that the reader has perhaps been wanting to make for some time: how *could* the musical example be perceptual by Fodor's lights? By 'perceptual' he just means whatever is modular; and that implies, among other things, diachronic encapsulation.

But this way of reading Fodor would be a mistake, I think. It would render more or less tautological the claim that perceptual systems are modules. And Fodor explicitly states that "modularity is an *empirical* thesis" ("Reply," p. 255). I take it, moreover, that what is asserted to be empirical here is not just the fairly weak claim that, somewhere in the mind or brain, there are modules, but the more substantive one that *perceptual systems* are modules. But if the latter thesis has genuine empirical content, there must be some independent constraint on what is to count as a perceptual system – independent of modularity – that lets us say that systems which satisfy *that* constraint are modular and, moreover, diachronically encapsulated.[29] This reading of Fodor is supported by the fact that he says

[29]Camilleri claims that experiments with interleaved melodies should be seen as confirmation, rather than disconfirmation, of "the thesis that no background information is accessed in what we call primary perception" (see Camilleri [1989], p. 38,

much to provide such independent constraint. (Actually, a notion of perceptual system independent of *diachronic* encapsulation is all I need for my purposes here; it would not affect the argument if we assumed synchronic encapsulation to be a constitutive feature of a perceptual system.)

We shall turn our attention in a moment to the way in which Fodor limns the notion of a perceptual system. But first a word about why this matter should be regarded as problematic in the first place. After all, the output of a perceptual system is just how things look (or sound, etc.). What could be clearer than that? Of course, we need to have a distinction between how things look and how we believe them to be, as the Müller-Lyer example shows. But when we understand that distinction, don't we have a perfectly adequate grasp of the notion of 'looks', and hence of 'perceptual'?

Things are not so simple, I believe. As Fodor points out, "The question where to draw the line between observation and inference (in the psychological version, between perception and cognition) is one of the most vexed, and most pregnant, in the philosophy of science"; there is a wide diversity of opinion on the matter (*MM*, p. 86).[30] The real question is why this *should* be a vexed issue, or why a disagreement over where to draw the line between observation and inference (or perception and cognition) is more than a mere terminological dispute. I view this question with some trepidation, since it seems to me to point to a central puzzle in the philosophy of perception. But it is relevant that our intuitions about appearance are slip-

---

citing experiments in Dowling and Harwood [1986], p. 127). Camilleri argues that since we are able to isolate the individual melodies on the basis of background knowledge and sufficient attention, our hearing of those melodies cannot be "primary perception." We should be suspicious of the ease of this argument: without more of an independent constraint on what is to count as primary perception, it is hard to see what prevents us from ruling out any potential counterexample to the given thesis. But if the thesis is immune to disconfirmation, it lacks empirical content.

[30]For a historical survey and discussion of the issues, see Hamlyn (1961); see also Heil (1983), p. 33, and Swartz (1965).

pery and unstable. We unreflectively assign certain semantic values to appearance – we say what the appearances are *of* – but when we reflect and try to distinguish appearance proper from what we infer from it, we tend to retreat from our initial assignments. On the one hand, it seems correct to say that a room can look empty, a brooch expensive, a car new, a defendant guilty.[31] On the other hand, it seems doubtful to claim that guilt is a visible property, that it is *seen* rather than inferred.[32] But these intuitions do not converge on any stable, core notion of appearance, something that would dictate in a clear and natural way what a purely observational language would be. We are, instead, left with a cluster of conflicting intuitions.

It is partly because there is no unique and stable intuitive conception of appearance, I think, that it has been so difficult to draw a principled distinction between appearance and inference. Since conflicting intuitions are at work, it is incumbent on Fodor to indicate which of them, if any, his own version of the distinction is meant to capture.

The Müller-Lyer example – which is prominent in Fodor's treatment – bears less weight for this purpose than one might think. Fodor uses the example to illustrate the distinction between appearance and belief. But that distinction should not be identified with the distinction between appearance and subsequent inference. Consider a situation in which you are perceptually presented with a defendant who looks guilty, but you are inclined to think that the entire perceptual presentation is illusory – perhaps you think you are hallucinating. It seems open to say that in this case 'guilty' is a term implicated neither in belief nor in perceptual hypothesis, but in some third thing: a nonperceptual hypothesis at work in central systems, something that is inferred from a perceptual hypothesis but does not sur-

---

[31]The last example is drawn from Harman (1973), p. 180.

[32]Cf. Berkeley's (1734) example of the coach: "In truth and strictness, nothing can be *heard* but *sound:* and the coach is not then properly perceived by sense, but suggested from experience" (p. 204, cited in Armstrong [1961], p. 19).

vive as a belief. This third category should have a more prominent role in Fodor's account. It is important because, if we neglect it, we are in danger of mistakenly collapsing the appearance–subsequent inference distinction into the appearance–belief distinction; and it is the former, not the latter, that is at issue.

4.5　Much of what Fodor says that is relevant to determining the boundaries of perceptual systems is contained in the section entitled "Input analyzers have 'shallow' outputs" (*MM*, pp. 86–99). Despite the title, Fodor wants to give a notion of perceptual hypothesis that is not too shallow, or too close to raw sensory stimulation. Examples of levels that are "too shallow" include early stages of visual processing such as Marr's "3 D" sketch (*MM*, p. 94).[33] In explaining why he wants to avoid too-shallow levels, Fodor invokes a criterion of "phenomenological accessibility" for perceptual hypotheses:

It may be thought Pickwickian, after all that we've been through together, for me to cleave to phenomenological accessibility as a criterion of the output of the visual processor. I must confess to being influenced, in part, by ulterior – specifically, epistemological – motives. It seems to me that we want a notion of perceptual process that makes the deliverances of perception available as the premises of *conscious* decisions and inferences; for it seems to me indubitable that, e.g., it sometimes happens that I look out the window, see that it is raining, and decide, in light of what I see, to carry my umbrella.
. . . [B]arring evidence to the contrary, it would be convenient if the output vocabulary of the perceptual analyzers overlapped the vocabulary of such (prima facie) perceptual premises as figure in conscious inference and decision-making (so that such remarks as "I see that it's raining" could be taken as literally true and not just enthymemic). Why shouldn't one assume what it is convenient to assume? (*MM*, p. 136n)

This passage states some important constraints on Fodor's conception of a perceptual system. Perceptual hypotheses are consciously available to the perceiver. They are at a "nonshallow" enough lev-

---

[33]See Marr (1982).

el to enter, without further translation, into ordinary reasoning about environmental conditions and action. The content of perceptual hypotheses will enter more or less directly, then, into commonsense intentional explanations of the sort that explain what people do in terms of what they see. Fodor's notion of the perceptual is specified, therefore, by reference to its role in (a certain kind of) psychological explanation.

Fodor expands on this notion of the perceptual by appeal to a construct of some currency in cognitive psychology, that of "basic" categories.[34] A category is to be understood here as an element of an implicational hierarchy, whereby anything that satisfies one element of the chain satisfies all the higher ones as well: Fodor's example is *poodle, dog, mammal, animal, physical object, thing* (*MM*, p. 94). A category is basic, according to Fodor, if it satisfies most or all of a certain set of conditions (which we shall consider in a moment); the categories that turn out to be basic by these criteria are, intuitively, "middle-level" categories – *dog* rather than *poodle* or *thing*. This, Fodor suggests, is the level of the vocabulary of perceptual hypotheses.

One of Fodor's conditions is that words for basic categories occur with higher frequency, and are learned earlier, than words for other levels (*MM*, p. 95). Another is that basic categories are ones we naturally use to describe what we perceive (*MM*, p. 96). As Fodor sees it, this points to an important fact: "Basic categorizations are phenomenologically *given*"; they have a certain "phenomenological salience." A third condition that Fodor states seems to me the most substantive, so let me quote him at length:

Basic categories are typically the most abstract members of their implication hierarchies which subtend individuals of approximately similar appearance. So, roughly, you can draw something that is just a dog, but you can't draw something that is just an animal; you can draw something that is just a chair, but you can't draw something that is just furniture.

This observation suggests that, to a first approximation, basic catego-

[34]Brown (1958) and Rosch et al..(1976), cited in *MM*, p. 94.

rizations (unlike categorizations that are more abstract) can be made, with reasonable reliability, on the basis of the visual properties of objects. . . . [T]he categorizations [input] systems effect must be comprehensively determined by properties that the visual transducers can detect: shape, color, local motion, or whatever. Input systems aren't, of course, confined to encoding properties like shape and color, but they *are* confined – in virtue of their informational encapsulation – to categorizations which can be inferred, with reasonable accuracy, from such "purely visual" properties of the stimulus. . . .

Putting it all together, then: basic categorizations are typically the most abstract members of their inferential hierarchies that *could* be assigned by an informationally encapsulated visual-input analyzer; more abstract categorizations are not reliably predicted by *visual* properties of the distal stimulus. (*MM*, pp. 96–7)

I am not entirely sure I understand how this appeal to implicational hierarchies is supposed to work, since, intuitively, it seems that the following can be the case: there is some category which subtends individuals of different appearance but is composed of subcategories each of which is homogeneous in appearance. Since membership in the more abstract category is predicted by membership in one of its subcategories (that is what it is to be an implicational hierarchy), the former *will* be predicted by "purely visual" properties of the stimulus. The condition that "basic categories are typically the most abstract members of their implication hierarchies which subtend individuals of approximately similar appearance" is not adequately glossed, then, by the condition that "more abstract categorizations are not reliably predicted by *visual* properties"; the former is stronger and, I take it, essential to Fodor's point.

As a *definition*, of course, it would be circular to explain what a perceptual hypothesis is via the notion of basic categories and to explicate that in turn by reference to individuals of "approximately similar appearance"; for it is precisely the notion of appearance that a perceptual hypothesis is supposed to capture. But we might regard Fodor's story not so much as a definition as an "intuition pump"; and it does do much to excite the proper intuitions, succeeding in specifying one reasonably clear sense in which we speak of phenomenal similarity.[35] It is reasonably clear what we mean when we say that, by and large, dogs look alike but animals do not. Phenomenal similarity in this sense is connected with certain facts about pictorial representation: it is possible to convey pictorially the common appearance that dogs share, whereas there is no such common appearance among animals to be portrayed pictorially.[36] And (if I grasp the notion right) this sense of phenomenal similarity is one in which it may be said that many of Vivaldi's concertos sound alike, but not all church music, say, sounds alike;[37] in which the Müller-Lyer lines do not look alike; and in which, in Goodman's well-known example,[38]

$$a \quad d \quad A$$
$$m \quad w \quad M$$

inscriptions of the same letter need not look alike (more than inscriptions of different letters do). Such examples point to a relation of phenomenal similarity that is real and important and – it is intuitively compelling to say – genuinely distinct from similarity in other respects. It is this notion of phenomenal similarity that, I take it, lies behind Fodor's conception of a basic category and, in turn, a perceptual hypothesis.

4.6   I want to summarize now the main aspects of Fodor's notion of a perceptual hypothesis. First, a perceptual hypothesis has a

---

[35]The term 'intuition pump' is due to Dennett (1990), p. 521.

[36]Conventionalist worries arise here: the fact that there can be dog pictures but not animal pictures might have more to do with our conventions of pictorial representation than anything else. But I think Fodor is right to resist this line.

[37]There was an amusing sketch some years back, on a popular late-night television comedy show, purporting to be a commercial for an album by Gordon Lightfoot. Though the titles and words of the excerpts varied, the music was always the same. The point of the sketch, of course, was that everything this singer does sounds alike. Phenomenal similarity with a vengeance.

[38]Goodman (1972), p. 438.

prominent role in conscious decision making and inference. Second, its terms are ones we naturally use to describe what we see or hear; they are phenomenologically salient. Third, it captures judgments of phenomenal similarity, of looking or sounding alike.

We are left with an inescapable conclusion. By the criteria stated, the effects of musical training are perceptual. A trained musician, listening in an appropriate way, will be conscious of whether he is hearing a tonic pitch or a dominant, a major triad or minor. A composer will make choices predicated on constraints he conceives of, and hears, in music-theoretic terms. Asked to describe how she hears a piece or passage, an analyst will produce an analytic description under which she hears the music. The elements of such a description will typically be phenomenologically salient, for trained listeners. Passages with similar descriptions will sound alike to such listeners: the latter will be able to distinguish reliably, by ear, passages that satisfy such a description from ones that do not.[39] The criteria that allow *dog* and *rain* to enter into perceptual hypotheses for you and me, then, allow *dominant* to enter into perceptual hypotheses for trained listeners.

It follows in short order that trained musical perception is a counterexample to the claim that perception is diachronically encapsulated, since the relevant effects of musical training constitute an augmentation of one's perceptual vocabulary, which means a failure of diachronic encapsulation.

Of course, there are any number of moves Fodor could make to resist the conclusion that trained musical hearing is perceptual in his sense. But it is hard to think of any that will not seem, at this stage in the argument, artificial. He might point to the requirement that words for basic categories are learned early and have a high frequency count. But in what population? To insist that it must be the general population would be an instance, if there ever was one, of begging the question; it would simply rule out the possibility – which seems

---

[39]I take discrimination to be a necessary condition for phenomenal similarity, although this is not explicit in Fodor, as far as I can see.

entirely conceivable – that a subpopulation can have extraordinary perceptual capacities. And how early must the words for basic categories be learned? To insist strongly on very early acquisition is again to beg the question, in this case that of plasticity. Likewise, Fodor might contend that the level of music-theoretic description is not "natural" or that the kind of listening appropriate for producing such descriptions is excessively inferential. But all of the behavior I have described is natural for a trained listener, or as natural, at any rate, as is its counterpart in everyday visual perception. A trained listener, when asked to describe what she hears, is apt to respond – spontaneously and without much ratiocination – in a way that employs theoretical terminology: she hears a piece under a certain music-theoretic description and will give that description in describing what she hears.[40] There is simply no principled basis on which to say that trained listeners do not hear chords as tonics and dominants in as full-blooded a sense as that in which ordinary perceivers see tables and chairs; or, at any rate, if there is a basis for saying this, Fodor has not told us what it is.

Of course, as we noted earlier, it is open to Fodor to stipulate some other notion of perception (and observation) that renders his argument immune to the counterexample of trained musical perception; he might, for example, simply stipulate that whatever is perceptual *must* be diachronically encapsulated, thus ruling any potential counterexample out of court. But by now such a stipulation will seem artificial, and the resulting thesis uninteresting. Fodor is absolutely right to understand perception in terms of the explanatory role he assigns it – phenomenological salience, entering into decision making, and so on. The interesting question is whether perception in *this* sense is encapsulated and leads to a viable attendant distinction

---

[40]There may be a mismatch between the scale of detail the describer uses and what she perceives – e.g., she may say, 'I am hearing a recapitulation' instead of 'I am hearing a minor triad'. But this point affects ordinary perception as well: though (to borrow Fodor's example) I may say, 'I see a lady walking a dog', it does not follow that I do not see the color of her gloves (cf. *MM*, p. 96).

between observation and theory. (Whether there are modular, diachronically encapsulated mental processes that do not fill this role is beside the point; there may be such, but they are not perception in the relevant sense.)

I want to consider one other line of response open to Fodor. This response would take the form of denying that the musical case involves a failure of diachronic encapsulation, because the effects of musical training are a development *within* a perceptual module rather than penetration from without. Fodor does allow that there may be growth, and a certain limited amount of plasticity, internal to modules.[41] (A limiting case of this response would be that musical training activates a vocabulary innate in the listener.)

But it is not clear how this line can be of any use to one looking to perception as a source of theory neutrality. If a perceptual module can develop internally, and thereby generate a music-theoretic vocabulary, what reason do we have to think it cannot generate arbitrarily many other vocabularies? It is hard to see how any useful notion of theory neutrality remains. And the situation is no better if we suppose the relevant vocabulary to be innate: if certain elementary music-theoretic terms are already specified somehow in the perceptual modules of untrained listeners, what else may be lurking there? Atonal set theory? Quantum physics?

Saying that modules develop from the inside rather than being affected from the outside would thus be a strategy of little help to Fodor. It does not explain away the basic phenomenon: the richness of a trained listener's perceptual vocabulary, which is enough to disqualify such hearing as theory-neutral observation. There should be no solace for Fodor in the idea that a perceptual module learns mu-

---

[41]I am indebted to David Temperley for pressing the point that, on Fodor's view, modules can grow or "learn" (personal communication). It should be noted, however, that in some cases Fodor considers such learning to involve intramodular plasticity, e.g., the inverting-lens case ("Reply," pp. 258–9), whereas he takes others to be instances of diachronic penetration, e.g., language acquisition ("OR," p. 248).

sic theory on its own, or always knew it: it knows it now, and it knows too much.

4.7 Having based the preceding argument on what I hope has been a close and reasonably sympathetic reading of *The Modularity of Mind*, I want to express some doubt about whether that account should, after all, be looked to as a source of anything decisive for the debate over plasticity and theory-neutral observation. My reservations stem from Fodor's reply to Churchland on the topic of reading. I give first the relevant passage from Churchland and then Fodor's reply:

[Churchland]: In recent centuries [we] have learned to perceive speech not just auditorally but visually: we have learned to read. . . . [T]he eyes . . . were [not] evolved for the instantaneous perception of those complex structures and organizations originally found in auditory phenomena, but their acquired mastery here illustrates the highly sophisticated and decidedly supernormal capacities that learning can produce in them.[42]

[Fodor]: In recent centuries we have learned to perceive automobiles (not just aurally, but visually). Now the eyes were not evolved for the instantaneous perception of those complex structures. So doesn't their acquired mastery illustrate the highly sophisticated and super-normal capacities that learning can produce in perception?
. . . Churchland needs, and doesn't have, an argument that the visual perceptual capacities of people who can read (or, mutatis mutandis, people who can automobile-spot) differ in any interesting way from the visual perceptual capacities of people who can't. In precisely what respects does he suppose illiterates to be *visually* incapacitated?
   The old story is: you read (spot automobiles) by making educated inferences from properties of things that your visual system *was* evolved to detect; shape, form, color, sequence, and the like. Churchland offers no evidence that educating the inferences alters the perceptual apparatus. ("Reply," p. 259)

---

[42]Churchland (1988), p. 177; quoted in "Reply," p. 259.

It is difficult to reconcile this estimation of the perceptual contents we actually enjoy with the position taken in *The Modularity of Mind*. There, the view is that "input systems aren't confined to encoding properties like shape and color," but can encode categorizations at the level of ordinary objects (dogs and rain) (*MM*, pp. 97, 136n).[43] The "old story" Fodor invokes in "Reply," then, is quite different from the modularity story. And they differ on the crucial point, moreover, of where ordinary objects are located relative to the distinction between observation and subsequent inference. In the modularity account, the level of ordinary objects is observational; in "Reply," it is postobservationally inferential.

How shall we interpret Fodor at this point? Perhaps he has changed his mind about perceptual systems. Or perhaps in his response to Churchland, Fodor is not talking about perceptual hypotheses at all, but has some other notion in mind. Either way, it is now difficult to see what we are entitled to draw from the modularity account as relevant to the plasticity debate: the question is not whether perceptual hypotheses as outlined in the modularity account can be theory-laden, but whether states that are perceptual in some stronger or narrower sense can be theory-laden. But if that is so, then an alternative or revised account would be demanded. Yet in "Reply" Fodor does not give, or even hint at a need for, such an account. He says nothing to retract his invocation of the modularity story as the foundation for the argument for theory neutrality ("OR," pp. 244–5).[44]

I see no alternative to the conclusion, then, that Fodor has simply stated an inconsistent position. He is driven to do so, I believe, because he wants a notion of perception robust (nonshallow) enough to enter into psychological explanations of decision making and action,

---

[43]Of course, it would not be plausible for Fodor to maintain that the examples should be treated differently, that *dog* is perceptual in a way that *automobile* is not. As dogs go, go automobiles; or the other way around, actually.

[44]Perhaps he gives a revised account elsewhere, although I am not aware of it.

but shallow enough to serve as a basis for a theory-neutral conception of observation. When Fodor sees that plausible candidates for the former will not do for the latter, he retreats to a narrower estimation of what is perceptual; but on pain of inconsistency, he cannot do so while maintaining allegiance to his earlier account.

The question is what we should now say Fodor must give up in order to avoid inconsistency. We will preserve more, I think, if we discount the narrower estimation of the perceptual given in "Reply" than if we reject the modularity account, since we have seen no independent basis for the former. The argument of the preceding sections, based on the modularity account, then stands.

4.8 In the remainder of this chapter, I want to return to the role of observation in rational theory choice and consider the impact of trained musical perception on that issue. I have pursued the questions about perception because I think that Hanson and his followers were on to something deep and important in asserting that seeing is theory-laden. And I have argued that modularity theory does not refute that insight.

Nevertheless, on the issue of theory neutrality, it does seem open to Fodor to argue as follows. *Some* process in the brain, beginning with sensory stimulation, is modular (where this includes being diachronically encapsulated), whether or not it is what we ordinarily mean by perception, that is, whether or not it is linked in appropriate ways to decision making and action, exhibits phenomenological salience, and so on. This module's output is semantically evaluable and is just what is necessary for a satisfactory account of rational theory choice in science. Moreover, this output is *all* that is necessary: we do not need to advert to anything inferred from those premises, anything more theory-laden, in an account of scientific confirmation. This, Fodor might contend, would provide just the desired notion of theory-neutral observation. And trained musical perception would not constitute a counterexample to this account, since

– he might argue – it is not the sort of observation that would enter, ineliminably, into an account of rational theory choice.[45]

The specific issue raised by this argument is whether trained musical observations ever play an ineliminable role in theory confirmation in music. A more general question is whether theory-laden observations relevantly similar to trained musical observations ever play such a role outside of music.

Fodor is interested mainly, of course, in the confirmation of *scientific* theories. And trained musical perception does not, as far as I am aware, play a confirmatory role in any scientific context outside of music theory – if, indeed, the latter is to count as science at all. Hence, as to the more specific of the two questions: even if trained musical perception does play a crucial and ineliminable role in the confirmation of certain theories of music, it would not constitute a counterexample to Fodor's view if those theories are not scientific. Nevertheless, Fodor would still have to contend with the more general consideration that observations *like* those of trained musical perception may sometimes enter ineliminably into rational theory choice in science.

I will not try to decide here whether music theory is science.[46] I want to argue, rather, that theory choice in music does sometimes depend on theory-laden observation, but that this fact poses no obstacle to seeing such choice as rational. To make the argument as relevant as possible to science, I shall frame it with respect to music theory construed along realist lines. I shall then consider briefly the analogy to (other) scientific contexts.

Let me say, first of all, what I mean by a realist construal of music theory. There are different stances that we can take toward the nature and perception of music-theoretic properties and toward theory

[45]This response exploits Fodor's stipulation that a module need not be "perfectly encapsulated," as long as it is "encapsulated enough to permit theory-neutral, observational resolution of scientific disputes" ("Reply," p. 255), though I do not know whether Fodor would countenance this line of argument (cf. "Reply," p. 257).

[46]On the claim of music theory to scientific status, see the next chapter.

acceptance. We might, for example, think of musical properties as subjective, and theoretical statements about musical works as neither true nor false, but accepted or rejected simply on the basis of interest, usefulness, or fashion. On this kind of stance, it is problematic whether rationality is an applicable notion, or at least whether a sense of rationality that would apply here would be strong enough for scientific contexts.

But to keep the discussion as close as possible to Fodor's (and Churchland's) concerns, I want to maintain a different kind of stance toward musical perception and theory, one I call realist.[47] On this stance, we think of the properties detailed in theories of music as belonging to musical passages and their sounded instances – rather than, say, to experiences or subjective states.[48] On this view, theories of music are empirical theories about structures or other properties of musical works, and musical perception is a matter of mentally representing sound-events as having such properties – in the case of veridical perception, detecting them.[49]

This stance is, at the very least, tenable. We might think of tonality, for example, as a structural property of a passage analogous to the way a physical object has a center of gravity.[50] And we might think of training in Schenkerian analysis, for example, as entailing the acquisition of certain observational powers – of detecting prolongations, diminutions, and certain other structural features that inhere

---

[47]This stance is essentially the same as what I called "representational" in Chapter 2.

[48]For a related discussion, see Chapter 6. There is a parallel with realist theories of color; see Hilbert (1987).

[49]A music-perceptual state thus has a truth value: it is true or false depending on whether it represents the sounded passage as it is. On a realist stance, a semantics for ascriptions of music-perceptual states is posterior to a semantics for music-theoretic terms.

[50]I have in mind Beardsley's discussion of tonality here, although I do not know whether he would accept the realist picture precisely as I have sketched it. See Beardsley (1981), pp. xxix, 105.

in passages of music.[51] Let us adopt this stance in what follows.

Do theories of music actually rely for their evidential support on theory-laden observations? I maintain that the answer is "often, yes." Claims about musical structure are commonly supported by the fact that the relevant structures can be heard in the music by trained listeners. Listeners' acceptance of such claims – and the rationality of that acceptance – depends on their being able to detect such structures. And higher-level generalizations or theoretical claims derive their evidential support in this way as well. For example, Schenker's theory of the *Ursatz* as a source of coherence for tonal music may be regarded as making predictions about observable structures in the music, predictions that can be confirmed or disconfirmed by trained listeners.[52]

What is absent from this account of confirmation in music theory is any counterpart to a condition Fodor apparently takes to be important for rationality, namely, that it is possible for scientists with differing theoretical commitments to agree on what would be relevant deciding experiments ("OR," p. 250). I call this the *condition of intertheoretic agreement*. Trained listeners are the measuring instruments in the case of music, and directly perceive auditory events under music-theoretic concepts. Untrained listeners do not have those observational concepts. Moreover, they typically do not have any alternative, nonobservational conceptions of the relevant properties (except, perhaps, under the description 'the properties that trained listeners are detecting'). Hence, there is an important sense in which they do not know what those properties are. The only way an untrained listener can fully understand and evaluate the relevant theory is to "go native": to study the theory, become trained, and learn to hear music under the relevant description.[53] This may be partly why there is less

---

[51]I am indebted to Naomi Cumming for a discussion of this point.

[52]Not to say that this is precisely what Schenker intended, but merely that it is a useful way of looking at his theory. See Schenker (1979 [1935]), p. 5.

[53]Cf. Kuhn (1970), p. 204.

consensus and communication in music theory than in the physical sciences: different theories or paradigms within music theory may require different sorts of perceptual training. Such training is apt to be lengthy and difficult, and different sorts of training may well be incompatible.

Of course, *some* observational properties are common to different theoretical perspectives in this sort of case. No one would deny that different listeners hearing Brahms's Fourth Symphony typically hear many of the same things. But those common observational properties are not by themselves decisive for theory choice. We should not underestimate the lack of commonality here. It is not as if different music theories can generally be understood as trying to explicate some theory-neutral, observational property such as coherence in a way analogous to that in which different theories of English syntax attempt to explicate grammaticality, a property neutral to those theories. (Rival theories in linguistics may be tested against intuitions about grammaticality that, presumably, do not themselves import notions specific to one theory or another.) Different music theories import very different notions of coherence; so the observations concerning coherence made from one theoretical perspective will often be incommensurable with those made from another perspective.

The condition of intertheoretic agreement – I take it – expresses the essence of Fodor's conception of theory neutrality. The question that arises in reading Fodor is just what the force of that condition vis-à-vis rationality is supposed to be. Perhaps he thinks of it as a necessary condition on rational theory choice, or perhaps he merely thinks of it as helping to explain what is rational in certain actual cases of theory choice. These postures should be distinguished. It may well be that the reasons we typically have for choosing one theory over another are based on data from experiments that adherents of either theory would agree to be relevant. If this is true, but insufficiently recognized – as Fodor seems to think – then he is right to point it out. It is certainly helpful to correct mistaken views about actual cases. However, it does not follow from any of this that the condition of intertheoretic agreement *must* be satisfied if theory choice is to be rational.

But I do think Fodor takes the condition of intertheoretic agreement to be a necessary condition on rational theory choice. He says that "the story about scientific consensus turns crucially on . . . theory neutrality" and suggests that an account of scientific controversy that does not advert to theory-neutral observation is likely to appeal to notions unable to capture the rationality of belief change, such as coherence or consensus ("OR," pp. 250–1). This implies that theory neutrality is needed to explain rationality.

What is difficult to see is why Fodor puts as much emphasis as he does on theory neutrality, as distinct from observationality per se. Fodor is "moved by the idea that belief in the best science is rational because it is objective, and that it is objective because the predictions of our best theories can be *observed to be true*" ("OR," p. 251). Sure enough, but this points to the importance of observationality, not theory neutrality. It points to the need for a distinction between the observational and the nonobservational, not between what is theory-neutral and what is theory-laden. There is no need to think that these distinctions are the same – that is, to suppose that what is observational, in a sense relevant to explaining rationality and objectivity, has to be theory-neutral.[54]

We may encounter a theory with certain observation terms that have no translation into our language. Observations in those terms, made by us (once we have "gone native") or others, may well enter into a correct explanation of why we are rational in coming to believe that theory. Music provides such a case: the fact that we can *hear* dominant–tonic relationships may well be a crucial part of our rea-

---

[54]However, aspects of modularity theory, minus the requirement of diachronic encapsulation, may well be relevant to explaining the observational–nonobservational distinction: an account of the distinctive epistemic role of observations may well advert to mandatory and fast operation, synchronic encapsulation, etc.

son for thinking that there *are* dominant–tonic relationships in the music. But it is observationality, not theory neutrality, that is doing the work in such an explanation.

I want to turn now to the scientific case and ask whether these considerations about music theory have implications for scientific confirmation. Of course, even if music theory is science in some sense, it operates at a different explanatory level than physics, and descriptions of musical structures do not occur in physics any more than color terms do.[55] If a realist conception of music-theoretic properties is correct, then such properties will at most supervene on, rather than be reducible to, physical properties. One might question whether the present argument carries over to the physical sciences, for which the issue of rationality arises with the greatest force.

Again, we have to distinguish the claim that theory neutrality *must* obtain from the claim that it often *does* obtain, in actual and important cases. The latter may well be true: it may well be that theory-neutral observation often does play an essential role in actual cases of rational theory choice in physical science. If so, and if we have been misled on this point, then Fodor is right to correct this mistake.

But *must* it play such a role, if scientific theory choice is to be rational? Consider a case such as the following, which is, in essential respects, no different from that of trained musical observation. A measuring device is developed, in the context of a new paradigm, that detects some property inexpressible, or which we do not know how to express, in the old theory. One might develop a gamma-ray detector, for example, a device that detects a phenomenon that cannot be described, or that we do not know how to describe, in terms of Newtonian mechanics. We may well be rational in adopting the new theory on the basis of observations made with that device, although Fodor's condition of intertheoretic agreement is not satisfied.

I expect Fodor would respond that his position does not mean to

[55]Hilbert (1987), p. 10.

113

deny the (rather unexceptionable) point that new measuring devices can be developed and that things or events that were formerly unobservable can come to be observable. But that is just what the condition of intertheoretic agreement denies. Or, rather, an insistence on that condition as a necessary constraint on rational theory choice amounts to a denial that new observations of this sort can play an ineliminable role in explaining why the acceptance of a new theory is rational. And it is hard to see why that denial is at all plausible.

The condition of intertheoretic agreement, understood as a necessary condition, is just too strong a constraint on rational theory choice. Perhaps, of course, I am wrong in reading Fodor as intending it to be a necessary condition. But then it is hard to see what the force of his insistence on the importance of theory-neutral observation amounts to: its role in an account of scientific agreement turns out to be much less "crucial" than he makes it sound. We may treat as a false dichotomy, then, the choice Fodor offers us between scientists' "fudging, smoothing over, brow beating, false advertising, self-deception, and outright rat painting" and experiments that can be evaluated from some theory-neutral perspective ("OR," p. 251).

4.9 For all I have said, modularity remains a fertile thesis about mental organization. But we should remember that there are many ways the story can go. We should be open to the possibility that mental faculties are modular in certain respects but not others. If what I have been arguing is correct, a perceptual system may be diachronically unencapsulated even if it is synchronically encapsulated. The kinds of semantic values had by the outputs of such systems may change, and we may come to perceive the world in new and expanded terms. Such a change in one's perceptual "vocabulary" may be brought about through exposure to and practice in a theory. Churchland is correct to point out a salient and important example of this phenomenon in music perception.

Much recent work in music theory and psychology has looked to modularity theory for a foundation. Although there is much to be said for exploring the relevance of modularity theory to music, the foregoing discussion has shown that modularity theory is underspecified in important ways and hence that its status as a foundation for music theory is not as secure as one might initially think. If Fodor can be indecisive about whether ordinary objects, as opposed to lower-level color and shape properties, constitute the vocabulary of perceptual hypotheses, then the very notion of a perceptual system is far from determinate. It may be that modularity theory should not be thought of as grounding music theory so much as depending on the latter for constraints on the notion of a perceptual hypothesis.

Fodor is concerned to argue for a conception of theory-neutral observation because he thinks it necessary to account for rationality in theory choice. His insistence on the importance of theory neutrality is, I believe, misplaced. It is observationality, not theory neutrality, that bears the weight here (and there is no need to conflate these notions). Rational theory choice in music supports this contention. Theory confirmation in music depends on theory-laden observations, and even if scientific confirmation often does not, there is no reason why it cannot.

What is at stake, then, in a debate over whether a given kind of musical hearing is perception or cognition? As I have maintained, the Churchland–Fodor debate derives its substance from the explanatory purposes to which the notion of perception is put to work. Fodor's modularity theory specifies one such set of requirements on perception: that it enter into the explanation of thought, decision making, and action at much the same level as ordinary talk of seeing and hearing. These requirements are amply satisfied by elementary, trained musical hearing, and this refutes the thesis that a perceptual vocabulary is insusceptible to enlargement from new theoretical perspectives. Trained listeners *hear* tonics and dominants, and perhaps even prolongations and diminutions, in as full and rich a sense as Fodor's modularity theory, not to mention ordinary discourse, could

115

want. For such listeners the appearance of music becomes "alter'd by the Judgment," and there is no reason to suppose that this is not a pervasive and important feature of perception in general. Perhaps it would be too much to say that music is a central part of humanity's epistemic adventure; but it would be a mistake to ignore what music can tell us about it.

5

Theoretically Informed Listening

5.1 Peter Kivy's book on musical experience begins with this epigraph:

It will be generally admitted that Beethoven's Fifth Symphony is the most sublime noise that has ever penetrated into the ear of man. All sorts and conditions are satisfied by it. Whether you are like Mrs. Munt, and tap surreptitiously when the tunes come – of course, not so as to disturb the others –; or like Helen, who can see heroes and shipwrecks in the music's flood; or like Margaret, who can only see the music; or like Tibby, who is profoundly versed in counterpoint, and holds the full score open on his knee.[1]

It is the difference between Mrs. Munt and Tibby that interests me and with which this chapter is concerned. Why should we, finding ourselves in the position of Mrs. Munt, aspire to that of Tibby? What are the benefits to a listener of having a technical knowledge of music? It is, of course, a basic premise of the program of aesthetic

---

[1]Kivy (1990a), p. vi; the passage is from *Howards End* by E. M. Forster.

education behind music appreciation classes that this sort of progress is worthwhile, but how and why is it so?[2]

This chapter is concerned in particular with the cast on these issues rendered by recent discussions of the *explanatory* status of music theory. In recent years there has been revived debate over the nature of theory, its claim to being a scientific enterprise, and its role in shaping musical activity and experience. In my view these discussions have tended to polarize the functions of theory as explanatory, on the one hand and as contributing to the listening experience, on the other, and laid insufficient stress on the way those functions interact. I shall argue here that the value of hearing music in theoretical terms sometimes derives from the explanatory potential of the latter and shall describe one way in which this can occur.

5.2 In their article "The Scientific Image of Music Theory," Matthew Brown and Douglas Dempster frame their discussion of the nature of music theory in the following way:

If music theory is to be taken seriously, and we think it should, then it must clarify the nature of music and thereby guide our musical activities, whether they be performance, composition or historical research. Music theory must also be a rational pursuit. By 'rational' we mean . . . that theory helps us illuminate, elucidate, understand or explain music. . . . Some [theorists] believe that music theory ought to model itself on the sciences; they claim that it can and should aspire to the rigorous methods and precise terminologies that have made science so successful in accounting for the world around us. They insist that it is only by applying scientific paradigms to well-defined phenomena, that music theory can be truly explanatory.[3]

Brown and Dempster point out two distinct roles or functions of

[2]The question is interesting partly because those able to listen to music analytically sometimes choose not to, but my topic here will be the benefits of theoretically informed listening, not why we might sometimes choose to do without them.

[3]Brown and Dempster (1989).

music theory: as an inquiry into music and "musical activities"[4] and as something that contributes to those activities. They go on to defend a conception of music theory as a scientific inquiry that aims at discovering laws of musical phenomena and providing Hempelian deductive-nomological explanations of those phenomena.[5]

Kivy devotes a chapter of *Music Alone* to the topic of music theory's claim to scientific status. His target in this chapter is the project of thematic analysis advanced by Rudolph Reti and invoked, sometimes implicitly, by other writers. The aim of thematic analysis, as stated by one proponent, is to "explain the musical as well as the psychological feeling of unity sensed in the great works of Mozart, Haydn, Brahms, Beethoven."[6] This is undertaken by reference to hidden, or at any rate nonobvious, thematic or motivic resemblances. Kivy compares this to the scientific goal of explaining the gross properties of matter in terms of its microstructure.[7]

Using Reti's analysis of Beethoven's Ninth Symphony as a paradigm of the approach, Kivy argues that it fails as science, since there are no clear constraints as to what is to count as a relevant thematic resemblance. Kivy goes on to suggest that such analyses are better understood along the lines of interpretation than as explanation: as

[4]I assume the relevant "musical activities" include listening, though Brown and Dempster do not explicitly say so in the quoted passage.

[5]Brown and Dempster (1989), p. 96. They point out certain ways in which the schema would have to be modified in order to accommodate a music-theoretic explanation, but their overall conception is in the spirit of Hempel's D–N model.

[6]Epstein (1979), p. 3, quoted in Kivy (1990a), p. 129. In *The Thematic Process in Music*, Reti remarked that the "existence [of the unity of a work may] be felt beyond a doubt," though "it may be difficult to prove" (1951, p. 355). This feeling of unity consists in, or is related to, the recognition that "we cannot produce a convincing musical composition by taking a group or a section from one work and linking it to that of another – even assuming an affinity of key, rhythm, and tempo" (p. 348). It was Reti's assumption that, although such unity is felt, its basis had not yet "enter[ed] the general musical consciousness" (p. 5) – whence his study.

[7]Kivy (1990a), p. 125.

Example 5.1

"open[ing] up to us heretofore unperceived and unappreciated features of the works they treat of for us to contemplate, understand, enjoy," in distinction to "explanations of [artworks] *qua* natural phenomena."[8]

Kivy's criticism may well be on the mark for the case he cites. Nevertheless, I want to suggest that music-theoretic terms typically do have a certain kind of explanatory status and that the value of hearing music in those terms sometimes derives from that status.

Let me illustrate the kind of explanatory connection I have in mind.

(1) Closure is explained by motion to the tonic. In the main theme of Haydn's Symphony no. 104, first movement (Example 5.1), the melody is relatively open or incomplete at certain points (e.g., on the second half of mm. 20 and 24), relatively closed at others (the beginning of m. 32). This is explained, in part, by the *scalestep positions* of the pitches. The tonic ($\hat{1}$, or do) generally sounds stable, the dominant ($\hat{5}$, or sol) unstable. Hence, motion to the tonic helps to explain closure, motion to the dominant a lack of closure.

[8]Ibid., p. 144.

120

Example 5.2

(2) A change in emotional tone is explained by a change in mode from minor to major. At the beginning of the fourth stanza of Schubert's song "Gute Nacht," there is a change in the mood of the song that might be described roughly as one from despair to nostalgia. This is explained in part by the change of mode.

(3) Unity is explained by motivic repetition. In a study paradigmatic of thematic analysis, David Epstein calls attention to the constant repetition of the ♩ ♪♪ rhythm in the Haydn movement just cited (see Example 5.2).[9] It seems to me that even if some thematic analyses ought to be dismissed as pseudoexplanation, the present

[9] Epstein (1979), pp. 143–5. Epstein points out all the instances shown in Example 5.2 except for m. 48.

121

case is different. The rhythmic recurrence does help to explain the unity or coherence of the movement, even as it sounds to a naive listener who does not attend to the recurrence. Or, at any rate, it is a plausible hypothesis that it does, a hypothesis that cannot be easily dismissed.

What I want to argue is that in cases such as this, the value to a listener of perceiving music in the relevant theoretical terms stems in part from their explanatory power. For us to see how this is so, we must first inquire into what is being explained in terms of what and into what the nature of the explanatory link is.

One possibility is that what is explained in these cases is a psychological state of the listener, or the event of his coming to be in that state. We might understand closure, on this account, to be a state marked by a lack of expectancy or a feeling of satisfaction. The relevant sort of explanation would then be a causal one, an explanation of how the music works on a listener.[10]

Surely there can be causal explanations of listeners' responses. But I want to suggest that for the cases in question another account is preferable.[11] For what is explained here seems best understood not as states or properties of listeners, but as properties of the music: one perceives the music as coming to a close, not oneself as having this or that expectation. Hence, if the phenomenology of musical experience is to serve as our guide here (as I shall allow it to do), we should understand the object of explanation to be the presence of a certain property in the music.

Let me suggest, moreover, that the explanatory relation here is not a typical causal one where cause and effect are distinct, but one in connection with the *reduction* of a property such as closure to theo-

[10]I am assuming that scalestep properties belong to the music and that their status is unproblematic.

[11]Kendall Walton (1993), pp. 262–4, suggests that music theory might be subsidiarily concerned with such causal explanations and considers how someone can appreciate the way in which music, or the telling of a joke, works on him. I do not rule this out, but explore a different option.

retical properties such as scalestep position. This follows Kivy's analogy of a microstructural reduction, such as that of heat to the motion of molecules. On the present account, then, the presence of closure is identified with some complex structural condition in terms of scalestep properties and the like. The explanation, on this account, depends on an *explication* of closure, an account of what it consists in.

Call this the *reduction model* of the explanatory connection, as distinguished from the causal model given earlier.[12] In my view, the reduction model is more plausible than the causal model in the present cases because the explanans and the explanandum are simply not distinct (or, at any rate, not *wholly* distinct). The event of a passage's coming to a close is not just something *brought about* by the motion to the tonic, but to some extent *consists* in that motion. The brightening in emotional tone of the Schubert passage is not just an effect of, but resides in, the change of mode. The unity of a passage is not separable from, but consists in, the various sorts of coherence that inhere in the passage: rhythmic, thematic, and so on.

The sort of explanatory power relevant to the present discussion, then, is that of explication and reduction – the reduction to theoretical properties of other properties that music has. And the central issue will be what this means for the listener. But first I want to address briefly two questions that arise about explanation and the status of music theory. The first is a skeptical worry about whether we have any reason to believe in such explanations; the second has to do with what role such explanations play in the music-theoretic enterprise.

On the first point, it might be argued that we do not have explanations unless we have laws; laws are exceptionless generalizations; and no one can actually state an exceptionless generalization linking, for example, closure and scalestep properties. Motion to the tonic is

---

[12]In his discussion of microstructural explanation Kivy cites John Searle's (1984) view that a "surface feature [can be] both *caused by* the behaviour of micro-elements and at the same time...*realized in* the system that is made up of the micro-elements" (quoted in Kivy [1990a], p. 125). I am not sure I understand this, but at any rate the reduction model does not exclude causation.

certainly not *sufficient* for closure, since the tonic can occur in the middle of a phrase; and it would not be hard to find examples showing that it is not necessary either. It would be difficult, in short, to formulate laws of closure.

But this does not show that we have no reason to believe that motion to the tonic has an explanatory link to closure. We can have reason to think a certain dependence exists without being able to state laws that govern it: we can see that the rock's striking the window caused it to break, even if we cannot say precisely which materials would break under what conditions. Of course, it takes *something* to justify such beliefs, but I would contend that experienced listeners have this, at least for the first two examples. (I am in some doubt about the third.)

The second question is whether it is a central task of music theory to provide such explanations and to discover laws that would support them. Now, if the causal model were correct, it would seem the relevant laws would be outside the domain of music theory. It is the psychology of music that is properly concerned with discovering laws of human responses to music, and we should no more conflate music theory with that discipline than we should conflate theories of linguistic structure with the psychology of language.[13]

On the reduction model, on the other hand (which we have adopted), it seems that music theory would *have* to be concerned with the discovery of the relevant identifications (assuming they are not obvious, so there is something to discover). If this is not the business of music theory, then of what theory? But it would still remain to be seen how important the discovery of such identifications would be, as tasks for music theory go. I will not attempt to answer that question here, except to indicate later on how an interest in such discovery may or may not be relevant to a listener's understanding.

5.3 Let me now ask what all of this means for Tibby. In regard to the first example, I assume that Tibby, by dint of diligent practice in

[13]Katz (1985), p. 203.

ear training, hears each pitch of the Haydn theme as having the scalestep position in D major that it in fact has. This means he can reliably identify the scalestep positions of the pitches he hears in this and unfamiliar tonal passages. Moreover, different pitches sound different to him in a way that is correlated systematically with their scalestep position. The pitch A has, for Tibby, the quality associated with sol in a D-major context; it does not have this quality in an E-major context, whereas B, the fifth scale degree in that context, does.

Mrs. Munt's experience, I take it, lacks this aspect. Hence, Tibby's experience has a content that is in some sense richer than hers. However, it is worth pointing out that this does not mean that the content of Tibby's perceptual experience is more *determinate* than Mrs. Munt's, in the sense that the truth conditions of Mrs. Munt's experience are wider, that it is satisfied by more possible situations, than Tibby's.[14] It may well be that Mrs. Munt's experience is just as restrictive in this sense as his. For Mrs. Munt's experience of the melody may in fact be a rather precise representation of it: she may be able to detect flaws in intonation and other mistakes. The important difference between her experience and Tibby's is that the latter has a conceptual dimension absent in hers. Someone might have a visual experience of a jagged mountaintop that represents it as having a certain irregular shape without possessing concepts to specify that particular shape. That perceptual experience would be one with a highly determinate "analogue," as opposed to conceptual, content.[15] Likewise, Mrs. Munt's analogue content might well be rich enough to determine the pitch content of the melody, on which the pitches' scalestep positions would supervene. Tibby's experience would then be better thought of as involving a kind of conceptual overlay on features already represented in Mrs. Munt's experience than as a more restrictive specification of how things are.

But with this clarification noted, the question remains: of what

[14]Saying that a perceptual experience is satisfied by a possible situation is equivalent to saying that it would be veridical in that situation.

[15]See Peacocke (1986). The example is his, in Peacocke (1992a), p. 111.

benefit is this conceptual level of hearing to Tibby? Let me say that the benefits in which I am interested are those of musical understanding and enjoyment. I am concerned, then, with describing how the explanatory status of theoretical terms is related to the understanding and enjoyment of someone who hears music in those terms. (That is not to rule out other possibilities for understanding and enjoyment.)

Here is one possible answer. Tibby knows that closure is explained by reference to scalestep properties. Hence, not only does he hear the music coming to a close, and hear the arrival of the tonic, but he hears the closing with an appreciation of the way it depends on the tonic's arrival. For this reason, his intentional object has a coherence not present in the experience of someone who is unaware of the connection. This coherence, moreover, leads to understanding and enjoyment: Tibby understands the music better in virtue of hearing it with an appreciation of the explanatory connection, and this issues in a more satisfactory, more pleasurable experience than he otherwise would have.

I believe this answer has plausibility. But two important objections can be made to it. The first is that it is not clear why we ought to count the understanding Tibby derives from knowing the explanatory connection as an understanding *of the music* rather than of how the music *is* or *works*.[16] Clearly, not everything that counts as a way of understanding an artwork in the latter sense is an aesthetic understanding or counts toward the aesthetic appreciation of that work. While a sensitivity to consonance and dissonance, for example, is surely essential to musical understanding, it is doubtful that a knowledge of their physical basis in frequency ratios is essential. We need

---

[16]This is, I think, the essence of a point made by Kivy in response to the preceding account, which was proposed in my comments on *Music Alone*. Kivy (1990b) questions whether on that account Tibby's enjoyment is an enjoyment "of the music" or "of the explanation" (p. 15) and links this to the traditional problem of "aesthetic or artistic 'relevance'" (p. 17).

some reason to count Tibby's understanding as an aesthetically relevant one.

The second objection is as follows. If our aesthetic posture toward a work consists in appreciating the way feature A depends on feature B, it had better be the case that one really does depend on the other. It is an important attribute of aesthetic pleasure that it is not merely hedonic, but has an aspect of being justified or grounded. A pleasure taken in the supposed way one feature depends on another, when it does not, would be a false pleasure and would entail no kind of understanding. (This would not be appreciation, but a kind of pseudoappreciation.) Moreover, it is part of the aesthetic point of view that we should avoid such false pleasures or misunderstandings. Now if, as appears to be the case, theoretical identifications of the relevant sort are not obvious, they would be appropriate topics for inquiry.[17] Hence, it seems as if the aesthetically appropriate attitude would include having an interest in being well informed about the results of such inquiry.

To put the point another way, theoretically informed musical pleasure, on this account, is subject to a certain defeasibility. Were we to learn that a given rhythmic repetition does not explain coherence, a pleasure taken in that supposed connection would be shown to be in a certain sense unjustified.

The problem is that the aesthetic posture taken in theoretically informed listening does *not* require this interest or involve this defeasibility. A concern with confirmation and disconfirmation – arguably central to science – does not play a comparably important role vis-à-vis the listening situation. (The point is not that we do not take this interest when perhaps we should, but that such an interest is not demanded by the aesthetic situation.) The pleasures derived from thematic analysis, for example, are immune from defeasibility, as they would not be if the foregoing picture were correct. The criticisms

[17]The point does not depend on this, but in my view the relevant theoretical identifications would be necessary a posteriori and the relevant inquiry would be empirical.

Kivy makes of Reti *qua* science are true, but somehow irrelevant. Kivy recognizes this, of course, and I take it that this is partly why he regards thematic analysis as interpretive rather than explanatory. But I hope to find a different way out of this box, one that captures the relevance of the explanatory aspect to the interpretive.

We might be led to a better account of Tibby's enjoyment and understanding if we consider the way the coherence of his experience was characterized earlier. One might, from the preceding account, think of his experience as consisting in an awareness of phenomenally distinct features that are, as it were, connected. By "phenomenally distinct" features I mean ones that are qualitatively different and introspectively distinguishable, such as the color of a patch from its shape, or the timbre of a sound from its pitch. It is, I want to suggest, an important fact about Tibby's intentional object that the relevant features are *not* phenomenally distinct in this way. The coming of a passage to a close and the motion to the tonic pitch are not separable aspects of Tibby's intentional object. Rather, the motion to the tonic, as he hears it, just *is* part of closure, as he hears it. Let me call this property of Tibby's intentional object, whereby the appearance of one feature is not (wholly) distinct from the appearance of another, *fusion*.

The present point is distinct from the basic tenet of the reduction model that the properties *themselves* (e.g., closure and motion to the tonic) are intimately related. The point is, rather, one about their modes of presentation to Tibby and consists in a stronger claim. For one might be presented with what correspond to the two sides of a theoretical identification via distinct modes: one might, for example, see in an electron microscope the motion of molecules that is the heat one feels. What is important about the musical case is that this sort of phenomenal separation does *not* occur: the intimate relation between the properties themselves is mirrored in the fusion of their modes of presentation.

Leibniz wrote that "the pleasures of sense are reducible to intellectual pleasures, known confusedly."[18] Theoretically informed listening, if I am right, is not always in the direction of decreasing confusion. Perhaps it often distinguishes what should be kept distinct, but sometimes it fuses what ought to be fused: as closure consists partly in motion to the tonic, so the appearance of closure, for Tibby, consists partly in the appearance of motion to the tonic.

I speculate – though it is a psychological question I am not prepared to investigate – that this fusion of qualities in Tibby's intentional object is sometimes a result of the fact that his perception is theory-laden. The more strongly someone believes that all and only *A*s are *B*s, the more the distinction between that person's seeing something as an *A,* and as a *B,* is blurred. It may be that a beginning theory student can identify motion to the tonic as such, and hear closure, without hearing one as part and parcel of the other. It may be necessary that one believe that motion to the tonic is connected with closure, and allow this belief to infiltrate one's auditory perception, for fusion to occur. That is the interesting case, so I shall assume this applies in what follows.

5.4   With the notion of fusion in mind, let me now make a revised suggestion about what is distinctive and valuable in Tibby's experience. Tibby hears closure for what it is. It is not the acquisition of an understanding of connections among distinct features he hears, but a deepened perception of a property for what it is, that is central to his increased appreciation. And with this comes a deepened pleasure in the music.

In the space that remains, I want to consider how this account fares against the two objections considered earlier. First, why should what I have described count as a deepened understanding *of the music?* I cannot offer a theory, from scratch, of what makes a way of listening to music an instance of musical understanding. However, it

[18]"Principles of Nature and Grace," cited by Kivy (1990a), p. 38.

does seem that, if the perception of a certain property is already recognized as basic to musical understanding, then hearing it in a deepened way is apt to count as an extension of that understanding. And closure and other properties explicated by music theory are typically basic to musical understanding. Of course, not *any* extension of perception based on a theoretical identification will do. Watching waveforms on an oscilloscope would not add much to the experience of pitch or timbre, or such is my intuition. But I want to suggest, though I cannot prove, that fusion is relevant here: it is the fact that we have an enrichment and extension of the experience of closure, rather than its supplementation by a different sort of experience, that makes theoretically informed listening particularly valuable.[19]

Let us turn now to the question about confirmation and defeasibility. On the present account, Tibby's pleasure is not one *taken in* the awareness of explanatory connections, even if it causally depends on a belief in such connections. This, I think, does something to defuse the second objection, since even if Tibby's belief is false, it does not follow that he is appreciating, or pseudoappreciating, what is not the case. So the interest we ought to have in avoiding such pseudoappreciation is irrelevant, on the present account.

Still, since on this account the way Tibby perceives a passage depends causally on his having certain theoretical beliefs, doesn't his aesthetic posture require an interest in being well informed about the truth or falsity of those beliefs, and isn't his pleasure defeasible? Suppose, for example, that he believes that the unity a naive listener senses in the Haydn is brought about by the rhythmic repetition and that this belief (inter alia) causes him, when he attends to the rhythmic repetition, to have a coherent and satisfying experience of the piece. Wouldn't the discovery that the rhythmic repetition has nothing to do with unity thus sensed rob his pleasure of a certain justification?

---

[19]As to why this leads to greater pleasure, I do not have a general account. It seems to me that the story in any given case would be parasitic on why the perception of the explained property is relevant to understanding and enjoyment.

In my view, the answer is negative. By the time Tibby has gotten to the point at which his listening strategy is coherent and satisfying, his enjoyment is likely to be aesthetically sound for many reasons unrelated to any such false belief. It may be, for example, that even if the rhythmic repetition has nothing to do with unity as the naive listener senses it, it has much to do with *Tibby's* experience of unity, since he has paid so much attention to it. The falsity of a theoretical assumption that plays a causal role in someone's arriving at a certain aesthetic situation will not undermine the situation, I suggest, if there are independent reasons for which it is to count as genuine appreciation. And this is, I think, usual in theoretically informed listening. For the listener, such assumptions are a ladder one might kick away; hence, it would be beside the point for Tibby to worry about their truth or falsity.

6

Conceptions of Musical Structure

6.1 Music, by most accounts, enjoys a vocabulary of technical description with a precision and expressive power unrivaled in other arts. It is generally admitted that the language of analysis allows a rich and detailed delineation of the structure of a musical work. Such descriptions draw upon intricate and elaborate theories of musical structure, such as Schenker's theories of tonal music.

The main questions I shall address in this chapter are the following: What is musical structure, of the sort described in music theory and analysis? What does it mean to say that this, rather than that, is the structure of a piece? What, if anything, do theorists who disagree over the structure of a passage disagree *about?* And what sort of thing is a structure, anyway? The present chapter is thus a philosophical inquiry into such matters as the form and content of structure ascriptions rather than a study within music theory that attempts to describe what structures certain works have.

First I discuss the logical form of structure ascriptions, making a distinction between strong and weak readings of such ascriptions. On the view I advance, ascribing a structure to a passage in the strong sense amounts to picking out a certain feature of the passage and asserting that the feature *is structural*. What makes a feature structural is the subject of the next section: I distinguish two main conceptions of structure, one whereby a feature is structural in virtue of its role as an object of perception or cognition, the other whereby the feature is structural in virtue of its having a certain kind of causal efficacy. In the last section I note how the existence of diverse aims of theory helps to account for the presence of diverse attendant notions of structure and urge that these distinct notions not be conflated.

6.2 Let me begin with some examples of the object of investigation. Consider the passage in Example 6.1a, which is the opening of Mozart's Piano Sonata in A Major, K. 331. According to the theorist Heinrich Schenker, the topmost melody of the passage is a prolongation, or elaborated version, of the stepwise descending line E–D–C#–B, or $\hat{5}$–$\hat{4}$–$\hat{3}$–$\hat{2}$ in A major. (Since the line begins with $\hat{5}$, it is called a $\hat{5}$-line.)[1] This conception of the structure of the passage can be conveyed graphically as in Example 6.1b.

Note that alternative readings of a passage are possible and can be the locus of debate among theorists. The Mozart passage, for example, might also be regarded as a prolongation of a $\hat{3}$-line (beginning on C#; see Example 6.1c).[2] The question is then: when theorists disagree over structural descriptions, what are they disagreeing about? What does it mean to say that a $\hat{5}$-line, rather than a $\hat{3}$-line, is the structure of the passage?

Let me turn now to a second example, drawn from the traditional roman numeral analysis of chords. A standard structural description

---

[1] The relevant prolongation operations are detailed in Schenker (1979 [1935]); analysis after Forte and Gilbert (1982), p. 134. The line is incomplete here, since it does not go all the way to $\hat{1}$, but this complication need not concern us.

[2] The motion to $\hat{2}$ at the end is a deviation I shall ignore. The foregoing interpretation essentially follows that of Lerdahl and Jackendoff (1983). For a discussion, see Peel and Slawson (1984), pp. 284–7.

Example 6.1

of chord (*) in Example 6.2 would be as a dominant triad, or V, in C (G–B–D; the E would be considered an ornamental tone). Again, an alternative reading is possible, III_6 (E–G–B with G in the bass; here the D would be ornamental). But most theorists would view the latter as an incorrect structural description.

We are concerned with such sentences, then, as

(1) P_1 (the passage in Example 6.1a) is a prolongation of a $\hat{5}$-line,

134

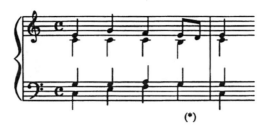

(*)

Example 6.2

and

(2) Chord (*) in P_2 (Example 6.2) is a V in C,

where these are read in such a way that one who accepts (1) or (2) may well reject

(1′) P_1 is a prolongation of a $\hat{3}$-line,

or

(2′) Chord (*) in P_2 is a III_6 in C.

The question is then how these sentences are to be analyzed. In what follows, I take it that they express facts of some sort, that someone who asserts (1) is saying that P_1 has a certain structural property and that someone who denies (1) is saying that P_1 lacks it. The question is then what sort of property this is, or what sort of "structural fact" is expressed here.[3] The main reason I take structure ascriptions to be truth-valued is that they enter into all the usual truth-functional contexts: it is usual for theorists to say that (*) is *not* a III_6; and at least some music theories can be stated in terms of truth-functional connectives, quantification, and so on, with structure ascriptions such as the foregoing as constituents.

[3]An alternative would be a "noncognitivist" construal, such as one on which the speaker expresses an attitude or recommends some action.

135

Example 6.3

But if we are to understand the language of structure ascription we must take note of a seeming inconsistency. Theorists are not entirely happy about calling (2′) *false*, for (as is plain to see) the simultaneous collection of pitches E–G–B is present. Nonetheless, (*) is not "really" a III_6, many will say.[4] Similarly, a theorist who prefers the $\hat{5}$-line reading of P_1 to the $\hat{3}$-line may not want to call the latter false, since (depending on how the operations are defined) the passage may well be generable from one line as well as the other. (Yet, such a theorist might say, P_1 is not "really" a prolongation of a $\hat{3}$-line.)

How are we to make sense of this? How can a chord be a III_6, but not "really"? (If we cannot make sense of this, so much for music theory's vaunted status as an articulate descriptive system.) Let me suggest that structural descriptions, or at any rate many of them, are systematically ambiguous. The point can be made clearest with a simple example (Example 6.3). Consider

(3) P_3 (the passage in Example 6.3) is made up of four groups of three notes,

and

(3′) P_3 is made up of three groups of four notes.

(3) can be read as equivalent to

(3w) P_3 is a mereological sum of four groups of three notes,

and on this reading someone who accepts (3) is apt to accept (3′) as

---

[4]Kivy uses "really" with this kind of force in (1990), p. 138.

well. Let me call this the *weak* reading. But there is clearly a sense, central to the whole enterprise of music-theoretic structure ascription, on which P_3 is "really" structured as four threes and not three fours. Call this the *strong* reading. (The strong reading is what we are centrally concerned with understanding here.)

Now, I want to suggest that (many) music-theoretic structure ascriptions admit of strong and weak readings. The weak reading of (1) is that P_1 is *generable from* a $\hat{5}$-line, whereas the strong reading of (1) asserts something more. (Hence, it may well be that (1′) is true on the weak reading though false on the strong reading.) (2), on the weak reading, asserts something such as that the pitches of (*) *belong to* the triad G–B–D; on the strong reading, it asserts something more.

We can gain further insight into the matter if we take note of a way we commonly make it clear that the strong reading is intended, namely, if we talk in terms of "functioning as." We are apt to say, for example, that chord (*) is (in the weak sense) a III_6, but that it does not *function as* a III_6, but rather as a V. What this suggests is that the weak reading of a structure ascription simply ascribes a certain feature to a passage, whereas the strong reading says not only that the passage has this feature, but that the feature plays some special role. Chord (*) *is* an ornamented E–G–B and *is* an ornamented G–B–D; but its *being* an ornamented G–B–D plays a role that being an ornamented E–G–B does not. The chord's being an ornamented G–B–D is a feature that *is structural* in this context, in other words, whereas its being an ornamented E–G–B is not. That is why (2′) is false on the strong reading though true on the weak.[5]

Now, it may well be that not every case of structure ascription in music theory fits the model just given. Pitch orientation, for example – assigning a home pitch or a fortiori a key to a passage – does not obviously admit of a strong–weak ambiguity, at least as far as I can see. Nonetheless, what I propose to do here is to explore the sort of

[5]The "functions as" terminology is not strictly synonymous with the strong reading, since we sometimes want to say that something that is not an *F* functions as one. I shall ignore this complication.

case that does fit the present model, leaving exceptions for another occasion.

To summarize the model, then. On the weak reading, a structure ascription predicates some feature F of a passage (chord, etc.); on the strong reading, it says that the passage functions as an F – or that F, as it occurs in the passage, is structural. The question is then what it is to function as an F, or what relation there is, if any, between being an F and functioning as one. The point I shall make is that, while there are systematic connections to be described, music-theoretic notions of structure and "functioning as" are basically heterogeneous. My concern in the next section will be to sketch what I think are the two most important such conceptions.

But let me make one point clear before I proceed. I have invoked the notion of the *role* (or roles) into which properties that deserve the name 'structure' enter, which is to say I have suggested a functionalistic account of structure. But I do not assume that such functional roles have to be described or conveyed entirely *within* music theory. I do not assume, that is, that music theory tells us *what it is* for a passage to have a certain structure, as contrasted with, for example, telling us how certain passages correspond systematically with certain structures or what laws govern structure. It may be that some music theories do the former, but there is no need to confine our notion of functional role to those within music theory.

6.3   The question I turn to now is this: in virtue of what is a feature structural? In my view there are two main ways of answering this, corresponding to distinct conceptions of structure relevant to music theory. The first is to be explicated in terms of intentional notions: on this conception, something's being a structure depends on its being a structure *for* someone, being apprehended or grasped by the mind. (Structure on this conception may be compared with meaning, at least as the latter is often analyzed.)[6] On the second con-

---

[6]See Loar (1981), p. 210. But see Harman (1987), p. 56, on calculation vs. communication and content vs. meaning.

ception, what is significant about structure is its causal role irrespective of whether anyone grasps or perceives it. Hence, the notion of musical structure is sometimes akin to that of the structure of a building in the sense conveyed by Nelson Goodman's phrase "how buildings mean"[7] and sometimes in the sense of "why things don't fall down."[8] As I shall outline later, these diverse notions proceed from diverse purposes of music theory.

6.3.1 The intentional conception.

On the first conception, structure is to be explicated in terms of intentional notions. The primary locus for this purpose is the listener and how she perceives the music (though it may also be relevant how others, such as the composer, think of the music, how they intend the listener to hear it, etc.). In hearing a passage, one has relative to one's auditory experience a certain intentional object: one hears the passage as having certain properties. (The intentional object is to be contrasted with the real object; among other things, the former but not the latter is incomplete.) A property's being structural, accordingly, derives on this conception from its being perceived, that is, its being included in the listener's intentional object. In other words, a passage's functioning as an F is to be explicated in terms of its being perceived as an F. This is essentially a phenomenological analysis of structure.

A simple theory along these lines might go as follows:

(4) F (in passage W) is structural iff a listener of kind K would perceive W as F.

On this view, P_1 has the structure $\hat{5}$–$\hat{4}$–$\hat{3}$–$\hat{2}$ in virtue of being perceived *as* $\hat{5}$–$\hat{4}$–$\hat{3}$–$\hat{2}$; P_3 has the structure four groups of three in virtue of being perceived *as* four groups of three; and so on. (Curiously, what makes chord (*) "really" a V is that it is *apparently* one.)[9]

[7] See the chapter "How Buildings Mean" in Goodman and Elgin (1988), pp. 31–48.

[8] See Gordon (1978).

[9] An account of pitch orientation might be given along these lines, in terms of a

The account just given amounts to a dispositional theory of structure, one on which a passage has a certain structure in virtue of having a disposition to bring about a certain response in the listener, namely, a cognitive or intentional state directed toward that structure. One is apt to notice the analogy with traditional accounts of secondary qualities, but note that the present view avoids certain difficulties associated with them. A dispositional theory of *red* is standardly given in terms of *looking red;* and then either we have what I call an intentionalistic circularity, on which a property is defined in terms of intentional states directed toward that very property, or else 'looks red' is to be taken to be semantically indivisible, in which case we are apt to postulate "sensational," rather than representational, properties of experience.[10] Neither untoward consequence occurs here, since strong and weak levels are distinguished: the property that *is* a structure is distinguished from its *being structural.* Consequently, the latter is defined in terms of intentional states directed not toward itself, but toward the former.

Now the account just sketched can be filled in or amended in various ways. One item that remains to be specified is the relevant sort of listener. We might want to take into account the fact that the composer has written for a certain actual, historically determinate audience (say Leipzig churchgoers of 1750) or, in the case of certain recent composers, has a particular kind of listener in mind (who may, with the exception of the composer, not yet exist).[11] We might want to put in a restriction to sensitive, adept listeners who have satisfying experiences of the music in question. Or the relevant notion in the dispositional account might not be that of a property's being perceived, but of its being perceived in a certain way. What is relevant

listener's propensity to hear the pitches of a passage as bearing certain relations, such as intervals, to the home pitch.

[10]Each of these has been regarded as a difficulty by some philosophers. See Smith (1986) and Peacocke (1983), p. 28.

[11]See Babbitt (1958), p. 38.

may be not that the work is perceived as having a certain tempo, but that the tempo strikes the listener as unusually fast.[12]

However these details are to be worked out, it remains that what is central to the account is that structure is something to be *heard*. Does this interpretation of theory and analysis square with practice? In my view it does; or at any rate it is a good first approximation to the practice of certain kinds of analysis. In such cases, analysts seem to rely primarily on the introspection of the objects of their listening experience in arriving at structural descriptions. Or rather: however they arrive at such descriptions, the test for their *validity* seems bound up with how the music is heard. This is particularly true of Schenkerian analysis, in my experience: the teacher with whom I studied Schenkerian analysis seemed to speak interchangeably of the sketches I wrote and "how [I] heard" the music.[13]

Let me point out one respect, however, in which the story might be made more complicated. We might want to preserve the idea that the notion of structure is bound up with that of what we can hear, while giving up the assumption that the structure of a given passage is to be defined in terms of what we can hear *in that passage*. That is, we might give up the idea of trying to define structure in terms of the listener's response, *considering each passage one at a time*. It might sometimes be correct to count a feature in a particular context as structural because of our more general capacities for listening and organizing our experience of music, even if in that context the feature is inaudible because we are unable to exercise those capacities fully. An occurrence of a fugue subject in an inner voice, for example, might count as a structurally relevant feature because of our recognitional abilities for melody generally, even if the particular occurrence is difficult to detect. (The analogy is with meanings or syn-

---

[12]Or as "contrastandard," in Kendall Walton's terminology. See (1970), p. 339.

[13]This need not commit us to an egoistic theory of the semantics of analysis: how a theorist hears a passage may be taken as evidential rather than constitutive of what an analysis means.

tactic structures too complex to understand, yet nonetheless deter-minate.)

This raises questions about the nature of music theory parallel to the recently discussed issue of whether linguistics is properly under-stood to be a branch of psychology. Jerrold Katz, for one, has argued in response to Chomsky's program for linguistics that a theory of lin-guistic *competence*, or of someone's *knowledge* of linguistic structure, is not to be conflated with a theory of that structure.[14] Scott Soames, likewise, has argued that linguistic theory is both "conceptually dis-tinct" and "empirically divergent" from the psychology of lang-uage.[15] Concerning music, Lerdahl and Jackendoff have explicitly favored a psychologistic interpretation of their own theory, along with a parallel conception of linguistics:

Linguistic theory is not simply concerned with the analysis of a set of sentences; rather it considers itself a branch of psychology, concerned with making empirically verifiable claims about . . . language. Similarly, our ultimate goal is an understanding of musical cognition, a psycholog-ical phenomenon.[16]

Should we go along with them as far as music theory is con-cerned? Let me remark first that later in this chapter I shall point out a kind of structure that does *not* depend on being an object of cogni-tion; hence, even if some music theory is psychological, not all is. Second, the analogy with syntactic structure noted earlier gives us room to retreat from a conception of music theory as a theory of what a listener hears in a passage, though continuing to think of structure as basically deriving from facts about what the listener per-ceives. The idea is that our perceptual or recognitional abilities con-sidered in general, not just case by case, might furnish a basis for the systematic attribution of structure.

I certainly do not want to maintain that this idea is straightfor-

[14]Katz (1985), p. 203.
[15]Soames (1984), p. 155.
[16]Lerdahl and Jackendoff (1983), p. 6.

ward or unproblematic. The crucial question is how our abilities are supposed to project to instances beyond our competence. Compositionality seems to be the key in the linguistic case, and perhaps it is relevant to the musical case as well. A musical structure may be built up in some sense from more basic properties or relationships – for example, tonic and dominant. But a problem that arises here is that of knowing when to stop, when the projection to further cases becomes unwarranted. This arises specifically in the case of Schenkerian analysis: many listeners report that configurations that occur (in their experience) on lower structural levels seem to lose their meaning when applied to higher ones. One might hear a phrase as $\hat{5}$–$\hat{4}$–$\hat{3}$–$\hat{2}$, but it is difficult to hear a progression such as this over the course of a movement. At what point does the ascription of large-scale structures to extended passages lose its sense? Does this point coincide with that at which one no longer hears such structures, or does it lie beyond? I am uncertain how this is to be answered in a principled way.[17]

6.3.2 The causal conception.

So far we have considered a notion of structure on which structure is something to be grasped. I now wish to contrast this conception with one on which it is a property's location in the *real* object, rather than the intentional object, that determines its being structural.[18]

[17] Before going on to the next section, let me mention a special case. The motivating thought on the present conception has been that structure is meaning-*like*. A welcome version of this idea would be that structure really *is* a kind of meaning. This view is taken by Goodman and Elgin (1988), p. 69, who hold that a variation exemplifies, and hence refers to, certain of its properties, including ones it shares with its theme. Insofar as music theory is concerned with structure in a sense in which theme and variation have the same structure, Goodman's explication of variation via semantic notions strikes me as potentially fruitful for the understanding of certain kinds of music-theoretic structure. A semantically based view of musical relationships can also be found in Kuhns (1978).

[18] Clearly, a feature must *exist* in order to enter into causal relations, and it is neither necessary nor sufficient for entering into those relations that it be *perceived*.

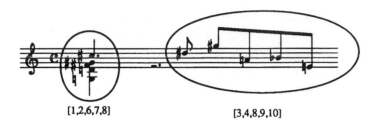

[1,2,6,7,8]   [3,4,8,9,10]

Example 6.4

The main problem with the phenomenological analysis of (certain kinds of) music theory is that it seems psychologically incorrect. Consider "set-theoretic" analyses of atonal music along the lines of Allen Forte's taxonomy (Example 6.4).[19] Such analyses segment a passage into collections of pitches systematically related to one another by inclusion, transposition, and so on. (In the present example, the second set is obtained by transposing the first up a whole step.) There is experimental evidence that such relationships are inaudible to normal listeners.[20] (This does not preclude the possibility that Forte's theory models what some *elite* listener hears, but it seems doubtful that this captures the real value of the theory.) There is also the example of Golden-Mean analysis: such proportions pervade the music of Bartók, but it seems unlikely that a listener can (or should) hear sections of a piece *as* 0.62 as long as other sections.

Of course, it is always open to us to interpret such theories and analyses as attempts to model the perceptual – just botched ones. But the principle of charity, as a canon of interpretation, dictates that we look elsewhere, and it seems plausible to think that these analyses get their point from certain causal powers of the relevant musical properties.

The idea emerges most clearly with traditional descriptions of form. Consider, for example, the form of Guillaume de Machaut's

[19]Forte (1973).
[20]Gibson (1986).

144

Example 6.5

chanson "Douce dame jolie" (Example 6.5), which features a pattern of repetition of text as well as music, as follows: *A bbaA ccaA . . .
qqaA* (where *A* designates the occurrence of the initial refrain with
the same words and music, *a* the same music with different words).[21]
As we listen to the chanson, are we, or need we be, aware of it as *A
bbaA* (etc.)? There are two ways of understanding the question, and
on each the answer is no. First, one need not have a synoptic grasp
of the whole in anything like the way one typically takes in all of a
painting at once; second, one need not hear the parts of the song in
relation to some plan one has in mind.[22] Yet the point of the structure ascription may well derive from the fact that the aesthetic qualities of the chanson depend on its having this formal arrangement.
There is likely to be a psychological explanation for this such as the
following. The listener is apt to become fatigued by hearing the same
melody and text over and over, but at the same time will be overly
taxed by constantly new material; this plan strikes the proper bal-
ance. (As a consequence, the eventual recurrence of *A* delights the

[21]Notated version after Schrade (1956), Second Part, p. 168. The given pattern is
that of a *virelai*, one of the medieval *formes fixes*. The point made here applies also to
rondo, bar form, etc.

[22]Though, of course, one *may*, but that does not seem to me to capture the real
significance of the formal analysis. I have profited from Levinson's (1993) discussion
of the views of Edmund Gurney and from the discussion of cohesiveness in Harris
(1988), p. 50.

Example 6.6

listener and somehow seems right and inevitable.) The point, of course, is that nothing in this explanation requires that the plan itself be an intentional object for the listener.

Although Schenkerian analysis often appears to be best understood along phenomenological lines, perhaps in some cases it should be looked at in terms of the current model. Concerning the analysis of the Mozart passage (Example 6.6), note that there is an identity in pitch between the first three pitches of the large-scale descent, E–D–C#, and the second, third, and fourth pitches of m. 4. Immediately after the large-scale descent has occurred, it is repeated more quickly – or "mirrored in the small," as Schenkerians would say. Though one might deny that when one hears m. 4 one hears those notes *as being identical* in pitch to the large-scale descent – since one's perceptual powers may not extend to comparisons among structural levels – it would be consistent to assert that the fact that this identity holds helps to explain what is elegant about the passage. It may well be that one's having heard the large-scale descent has an effect on one's hearing of the notes in m. 4 because they are the same in pitch. The latter pitches may well sound right *because* they have already occurred, albeit in large-scale form; and the unity or coherence of the passage may well derive, in part, from this identity. If so, what is important is that the identity is *there* and helps to explain coherence, even if the identity itself is unperceived.[23]

---

[23]Another analyst whose work might be understood on the current model is Rudolph Reti, who finds heretofore unsuspected thematic connections among move-

Hence, on the second conception a feature F is structural by virtue of F's causal powers, in particular ones between formal arrangements and our perception of aesthetic properties such as cohesiveness, unity, and rightness.[24] There are possible variants to this account: perhaps the relevant notion should be the dependence of aesthetic properties themselves, rather than our perception of them, upon structure. In this case, the dependence would perhaps not be causal, though it would still be explanatory in some sense.[25] However, for present purposes, I shall continue to call the account "causal."

In any case, I want to maintain that certain sorts of musical analyses are to be interpreted as proffering causal (or other) explanations of coherence or other aesthetic properties. But this does not mean that they must be interpreted as true or successful explanations. As Peter Kivy notes, music theory smacks of pseudoscience in this connection: in criticism of Reti, he points out that thematic analyses that purport to show the unity of a work can hardly be very revealing if the relevant constraints are so loose that virtually any re-

ments of a work, and even in what is generally considered contrasting material in the same movement. Reti says that a kind of "unconscious recollection" of earlier material occurs when one hears later, related material, and I take this to mean that what one hears later is familiar because one has heard the earlier material, not because one hears the later material *as* a repetition or transformation of the earlier material. Hence, it is plausible to understand Reti's approach as falling under the present model. See Reti (1951).

[24]More "local" perceptions might come into the picture as well – e.g., a chord might function as a V rather than a III because it is heard as having the tension normally associated with V.

In contrasting the present "causal" conception of structure with the intentionalistic conception, I do not mean to deny that perceptual notions themselves should be analyzed in terms of causality. What is relevant in the present case is causal powers *other* than those directly relevant to F's being perceived.

[25]I am not claiming that we should always understand music analysts as actually *giving* the relevant explanations. They might leave them implicit, or they might present data they think are *capable* of entering into such explanations, without having determined exactly how the explanations are to go.

semblance counts as relevant.[26] And another writer claims to present evidence that the order of movements of an extended work – hence, a fortiori, whatever structural relations supervene on that order – are irrelevant to (certain) listeners' aesthetic responses.[27]

Nicholas Cook's investigations into tonal organization are relevant here. Cook reports experimental results showing that normal listeners do not exhibit a statistically significant preference for pieces that begin and end in the same key over versions that do not.[28] He takes this to show that large-scale closure is unperceived, but allows that its aesthetic effects may be "indirect."[29] I take this to mean that he understands tonal structure along causal rather than intentional lines. Cook cites James Mursell in this connection:

We have [in tonal plans] a foundational structural factor without which effective relationships could not be established among elements of tonal content, and which are essential for the general architecture of music, its harmonic sequences, and above all for the writing of subtle and expressive melody.[30]

But in my view the crucial and interesting question is not whether a tonal plan is part of, in Cook's words, the composer's "abstract conception"[31] – which may mean merely that it serves as a propaedeutic to composition – but whether a certain counterfactual dependence holds, that is, whether the relevant relationships, subtlety, and expressiveness would not obtain if the plan were not present. And this, on my reading of Cook's results, seems more to be disconfirmed than supported by them. For he finds no correlation between tonal plans and aesthetic satisfaction, which weighs against the truth of

---

[26]Kivy (1990a), pp. 136–7 (see also note 23 above).

[27]Konecni (1984).

[28]This is true for passages of more than a minute or so in duration. See Cook (1987b), p. 203.

[29]Ibid., p. 204.

[30]Mursell (1937), pp. 215–16, cited by Cook (1987b), pp. 204–5n.

[31]Cook (1987b), p. 204.

the relevant structure ascriptions not only on an intentionalistic interpretation, but on a causal one as well.

Thus, I maintain, we ascribe causal–explanatory connections at our peril. But let me say that I think it would be a mistake for music theorists to allow their speculations to be inhibited by adhering strictly to scientific standards of confirmation. For they are mainly in the business of discovering and suggesting plausible hypotheses about how music works, not establishing them by scientific standards.

6.4   The fact that the notion of structure does diverse sorts of work is related to the fact that music theory has a diversity of purposes. Some of these purposes are related to the perception and appreciation of music, whereas others are concerned more with its production and technicalities. And within each of these areas theory can have the status of an inquiry, a pursuit after truth, as well as be important for its effects on composers, performers, and listeners. In what follows I have primarily the effects of theory in mind.

Musical analysis can serve as a means of communication among listeners, a way of sharing interesting features they have noticed with one another. It is thereby a means of transmitting interesting intentional objects. (This might happen indirectly, by way of a performer's projecting a certain intentional object revealed by analysis, making it available to be heard.) Moreover, analysis can contribute to the formation of new and interesting objects of listening experience. Two ways in which it can do so have been pointed out by Kendall Walton. First, features that are important for their causal powers – answers to the question "what makes this piece work?" – can *themselves* become items of interest to be perceived. That is, features that are structural in the second respect can become structural in the first. This does not obviate the distinction between the two conceptions, but means that there is a certain fluidity in what features belong to what category. Exploring music with this sort of

149

transformation in mind is of central interest to analysts of music.[32] Second, analysis can aid in the *recognition* of what one's intentional object is – becoming aware that it includes such-and-such features.[33] For reasons such as these, it is not surprising that the notion of musical structure is closely linked to that of the intentional object.

At the same time, other roles of theory in musical production and culture leave room for a wider notion of structure, one not limited to the intentional object but extending to the real object as well. A composer (writing in a certain idiom) will want to avoid parallel fifths not necessarily because they will be perceived *as* parallel fifths but because, all else being equal, such progressions are apt to strike the listener as ugly. The feature of parallel fifths is significant here for its causal properties.

I have been arguing, essentially, that we have divergent conceptions of structure: on the one hand, something to be perceived; on the other, something with a certain causal efficacy. The question arises whether these roles ought to be combined somehow into a unified account. We might thereby understand 'structure' not merely to express a conception internal to a particular theory, but to refer to an entity (or property) that lies behind a variety of theoretical purposes and conceptions.

It is relevant to consider in this connection views about music theory put forth by Matthew and Dempster.[34] The main thrust of their article is that, if music theory is to be a respectable discipline it must meet standards of explanatory adequacy appropriate for science. In the course of their argument, Brown and Dempster suggest that we think of terms such as *Ursatz* as theoretical in the sense familiar from the philosophy of science, rather than as operationally defined observation terms.[35] This (though it does not entail it) seems congenial

---

[32]This was pointed out to me by Marion Guck.
[33]Walton (1993), p. 266.
[34]Brown and Dempster (1989).
[35]Ibid., p. 96.

to the view under consideration, that structure is something that stands behind diverse conceptions of it held by theorists with diverse purposes.

I am skeptical, however, about the unity of structure. It is sometimes plausible to think of certain modes of inquiry as converging on the same entity: we think of heat as what feels a certain way to us, what causes mercury to expand, what causes ice to melt, and so on. But we need to have good reason to believe in such convergence, as we would if we had a truly explanatory theory on which a single entity is involved. But it is far from evident that we do; the situation, I want to suggest, is instead like the investigation of intelligence according to those who hold that intelligence is a matter of having diverse aptitudes and skills, not a single trait.[36]

There is no reason, as far as I can see, to think that different music-theoretic projects must have a common object of inquiry, one that detaches from the particular explanatory goals of any one such project. To be sure, music theorists do not always make this clear; and there may well be in use a notion of structure, as of intelligence, something like Wittgenstein's table that "stands on four legs instead of three and so sometimes wobbles."[37] But it does not follow that this notion is justified – that is, that we are justified in believing in some entity standing behind such a heterogeneous conception.

If we do not conflate what are in fact distinct notions of structure, moreover, we may avoid disputes at cross-purposes. I suspect that the question of whether triads and tonal functions are present in music before the eighteenth century is one such dispute.[38] To summarize the matter very briefly: those who answer this question in the affirmative point to clear instances of triads and root movement by fifth in the music; their opponents cite the theory of the time, charging that such tonally based analysis is anachronistic. It seems to me that much of the debate depends on an equivocation over intentional

[36]See, e.g., Gould (1981), p. 24.
[37]Wittgenstein (1958), p.37.
[38]See, e.g., the discussion in Schulenberg (1986).

and causal conceptions of structure. I hope to expand on this elsewhere.

6.5 Let me summarize the view of musical structure advanced in this chapter. Certain music-theoretic structure ascriptions point out a feature of a passage and distinguish it as structural. A feature's being structural can stem from either of two main sources: its role in the intentional object of a listener's experience, and its causal powers irrespective of being perceived. Both conceptions of structure must be recognized if we are to understand what the rich and intricate systems of music theory have to tell us.

Works Cited

Armstrong, D. M. (1961). *Perception and the Physical World*. London: Routledge & Kegan Paul.

(1968). *A Materialist Theory of the Mind*. London: Routledge & Kegan Paul.

(1973). *Belief, Truth and Knowledge*. Cambridge University Press.

Babbitt, Milton (1958). "Who Cares If You Listen?" *High Fidelity* 8(no. 2):38.

Beardsley, Monroe (1981). *Aesthetics: Problems in the Philosophy of Criticism*, 2nd ed. Indianapolis: Hackett.

Bennett, Jonathan (1966). *Kant's Analytic*. Cambridge University Press.

Bent, Ian (1987). *Analysis*. New York: Norton.

Berkeley, George (1734). *Three Dialogues between Hylas and Philonous*. In *Works*, ed. A. A. Luce and T. E. Jessop (London: Thomas Nelson, 1948–51), vol. 2.

Bharucha, Jamshed J. (1991). "Pitch, Harmony, and Neural Nets: A Psychological Perspective." In Peter M. Todd and D. Gareth Loy, eds., *Music and Connectionism*. Cambridge, Mass.: MIT Press, pp. 84–99.

Bigand, Emmanuel, Marion Pineau, and Fred Lerdahl (1993). "Two Experimental Approaches to the Components of GTTM." Paper presented at the Society for Music Theory annual meeting, Montreal, November 5.

Bower, Gordon H., and Arnold L. Glass (1976). "Structural Units and the Redintegrative Power of Picture Fragments." *Journal of Experimental Psychology: Human Learning and Memory* 2:456–66.

153

Brown, Curtis (1992). "Direct and Indirect Belief." *Philosophy and Phenomenological Research* 52:289–316.

Brown, Matthew, and Douglas Dempster (1989). "The Scientific Image of Music Theory." *Journal of Music Theory* 33:65–106.

Brown, R. (1958). "How Shall a Thing Be Called?" *Psychological Review* 65: 14–21.

Bruner, Jerome (1957). "On Perceptual Readiness." *Psychological Review* 64: 123–52.

Budd, Malcolm (1985). "Understanding Music." *Proceedings of the Aristotelian Society Supplementary Volume* 59:233–48.

Camilleri, Lelio (1989). "A Modular Approach to Music Cognition." *Interface* 18:33–44.

Carnap, Rudolf (1956). *Meaning and Necessity*, 2nd ed. Chicago: University of Chicago Press.

Chisholm, Roderick M. (1977). *Theory of Knowledge*, 2nd ed. Englewood Cliffs, N.J.: Prentice-Hall.

Chomsky, Noam (1957). *Syntactic Structures*. The Hague: Mouton.

    (1965). *Aspects of the Theory of Syntax*. Cambridge, Mass.: MIT Press.

Churchland, Paul M. (1979). *Scientific Realism and the Plasticity of Mind*. Cambridge University Press.

    (1988). "Perceptual Plasticity and Theoretical Neutrality: A Reply to Jerry Fodor." *Philosophy of Science* 55:167–87.

Cone, Edward T. (1968). *Musical Form and Musical Performance*. New York: Norton.

Cook, Nicholas (1987a). *A Guide to Musical Analysis*. New York: George Braziller.

    (1987b). "The Perception of Large-Scale Tonal Closure." *Music Perception* 5:197–206.

Crane, Tim (1988). "The Waterfall Illusion." *Analysis* 48:142–7.

    (1992a). "Introduction" to Crane, ed. (1992), pp. 1–17.

    (1992b). "The Nonconceptual Content of Experience." In Crane, ed. (1992), pp. 136–57.

Crane, Tim, ed. (1992). *The Contents of Experience: Essays on Perception*. Cambridge University Press.

Cumming, Naomi (1992). "Eugene Narmour's Theory of Melody." *Music Analysis* 11:354–74.

    (1993). "Music Analysis and the Perceiver: A Perspective from Functionalist Philosophy." *Current Musicology* 54:38–53.

Cummins, Robert (1989). *Meaning and Mental Representation*. Cambridge, Mass.: MIT Press.

Davies, John Booth (1978). *The Psychology of Music*. Stanford, Calif.: Stanford University Press.

Davies, J. B., and J. Jennings (1977). "Reproduction of Familiar Melodies and the Perception of Tonal Sequences." *Journal of the Acoustical Society of America* 61:534–41.

DeBellis, Mark (1988). *Music and the Representational Content of Experience*. Ph.D. dissertation, Princeton University.

——— (1991). "The Representational Content of Musical Experience." *Philosophy and Phenomenological Research* 51:303–24.

Dennett, Daniel C. (1969). *Content and Consciousness*. London: Routledge & Kegan Paul.

——— (1990). "Quining Qualia." Reprinted in William G. Lycan, ed., *Mind and Cognition: A Reader*. Cambridge, Mass.: Basil Blackwell, pp. 519–47.

Deutsch, Diana (1969). "Music Recognition." *Psychological Review* 76:300–7.

——— (1982). "The Processing of Pitch Combinations." In Deutsch, ed. (1982), pp. 271–316.

Deutsch, Diana, ed. (1982). *The Psychology of Music*. New York: Academic Press.

Deutsch, D., and J. Feroe (1981). "The Internal Representation of Pitch Sequences in Tonal Music." *Psychological Review* 88:503–22.

Dibben, Nicola (1993). "The Cognitive Reality of Hierarchic Structure in Tonal and Atonal Music." Paper presented at the Society for Music Perception and Cognition annual conference, Philadelphia, June 16–19.

Dolezal, Hubert (1982). *Living in a World Transformed*. New York: Academic Press.

Dowling, W. Jay (1982a). "Melodic Information Processing and Its Development." In Deutsch, ed. (1982), pp. 413–29.

——— (1982b). "Musical Scales and Psychophysical Scales." In T. Rice and R. Falck, eds., *Cross-cultural Perspectives on Music*. Toronto: University of Toronto Press, pp. 20–8.

——— (1993a). "Explorations in Melody and Tonal Framework." In Tighe and Dowling, eds. (1993), pp. 1–3.

——— (1993b). "Procedural and Declarative Knowledge in Music Cognition and Education." In Tighe and Dowling, eds. (1993), pp. 5–18.

Dowling, W. Jay, and Dane L. Harwood (1986). *Music Cognition*. San Diego, Calif.: Academic Press.

Dretske, Fred (1978). "The Role of the Percept in Visual Cognition." In C. Wade Savage, ed., *Perception and Cognition: Issues in the Foundations of Psychology* (Minnesota Studies in the Philosophy of Science, vol. 9). Minneapolis: University of Minnesota Press, pp. 107–27.

Epstein, David (1979). *Beyond Orpheus: Studies in Musical Structure*. Cambridge, Mass.: MIT Press.

Evans, Gareth (1982). *The Varieties of Reference*. Oxford: Oxford University Press.
  (1985). "Molyneux's Question." In *Collected Papers*. Oxford: Oxford University Press.

Fodor, Jerry A. (1983). *The Modularity of Mind*. Cambridge, Mass.: MIT Press.
  (1984). "Observation Reconsidered." *Philosophy of Science* 51. Reprinted in Fodor (1990), pp. 231–51.
  (1988). "A Reply to Churchland's 'Perceptual Plasticity and Theoretical Neutrality.'" *Philosophy of Science* 55. Reprinted in Fodor (1990), pp. 253–63.
  (1990). *A Theory of Content and Other Essays*. Cambridge, Mass.: MIT Press.

Forte, Allen (1973). *The Structure of Atonal Music*. New Haven, Conn.: Yale University Press.

Forte, Allen, and Steven E. Gilbert (1982). *Introduction to Schenkerian Analysis*. New York: Norton.

Frege, Gottlob (1956). "The Thought: A Logical Inquiry." *Mind* 65:289–311.
  (1980a [1892]). "On Concept and Object." In Peter Geach and Max Black, eds., *Translations from the Philosophical Writings of Gottlob Frege*, 3rd ed. Totowa, N.J.: Rowman & Littlefield.
  (1980b [1892]). "On Sense and Meaning." In Peter Geach and Max Black, eds., *Translations from the Philosophical Writings of Gottlob Frege*, 3rd ed. Totowa, N.J.: Rowman & Littlefield.

Gibson, Don B., Jr. (1986). "The Aural Perception of Nontraditional Chords in Selected Theoretical Relationships: A Computer-Generated Experiment." *Journal of Research in Music Education* 33:5–23.

Goodman, Nelson (1972). "Seven Strictures on Similarity." In *Problems and Projects*. Indianapolis: Bobbs-Merrill.
  (1976). *Languages of Art: An Approach to a Theory of Symbols*, 2nd edition. Indianapolis: Hackett.

Goodman, Nelson, and Catherine Z. Elgin (1988). *Reconceptions in Philosophy and Other Arts and Sciences*. Indianapolis: Hackett.

Gordon, J. E., ed. (1978). *Structures: Or Why Things Don't Fall Down*. New York: Plenum.

Gould, Stephen Jay (1981). *The Mismeasure of Man*. New York: Norton.

Hamlyn, D. W. (1961). *Sensation and Perception*. London: Routledge.

Hanson, Norwood Russell (1958). *Patterns of Discovery*. Cambridge University Press.

Harman, Gilbert (1973). *Thought*. Princeton, N.J.: Princeton University Press.
  (1987). "(Nonsolipsistic) Conceptual Role Semantics." In Ernest LePore, ed., *New Directions in Semantics*. London: Academic Press, pp. 55–81.
  (1990). "The Intrinsic Quality of Experience." *Philosophical Perspectives* 4:31–52.

Harris, Wendell V. (1988). *Interpretive Acts.* Oxford: Clarendon Press.

Heil, John (1983). *Perception and Cognition.* Berkeley: University of California Press.

Hilbert, David R. (1987). *Color and Color Perception: A Study in Anthropocentric Realism.* Stanford, Calif.: Center for the Study of Language and Information.

Idson, W. L., and D. W. Massaro (1978). "A Bidimensional Model of Pitch in the Recognition of Melodies." *Perception and Psychophysics* 24:551–65.

Jackendoff, Ray (1987). *Consciousness and the Computational Mind.* Cambridge, Mass.: MIT Press.

(1991). "Musical Parsing and Musical Affect." *Music Perception* 9:199–230.

(1992). *Languages of the Mind: Essays on Mental Representation.* Cambridge, Mass.: MIT Press.

Kallman, H. J., and D. W. Massaro (1979). "Tone Chroma Is Functional in Melody Recognition." *Perception and Psychophysics* 26:32–6.

Katz, Jerrold J. (1985). "An Outline of Platonist Grammar." In Katz, ed., *The Philosophy of Linguistics.* Oxford: Oxford University Press, pp. 172–203.

Kivy, Peter (1990a). *Music Alone: Philosophical Reflections on the Purely Musical Experience.* Ithaca, N.Y.: Cornell University Press.

(1990b). "Comments on Comments on Music Alone." Paper read at the American Society for Aesthetics annual meeting, Austin, Texas, October 24–7.

Konecni, Vladimir J. (1984). "Elusive Effects of Artists' 'Messages.'" In W. R. Crozier and A. J. Chapman, eds., *Cognitive Processes in the Perception of Art.* Amsterdam: North-Holland, pp. 71–93.

Kramer, Jonathan D. (1988). *The Time of Music.* New York: Schirmer.

Krebs, Harald (1991). "Tonal and Formal Dualism in Chopin's Scherzo, Op. 31." *Music Theory Spectrum* 13:48–60.

Kripke, Saul A. (1988 [1979]). "A Puzzle about Belief." In Nathan Salmon and Scott Soames, eds., *Propositions and Attitudes.* Oxford: Oxford University Press, pp. 102–48.

Krumhansl, Carol L. (1990). *Cognitive Foundations of Musical Pitch.* Oxford: Oxford University Press.

Krumhansl, Carol L., and Roger N. Shepard (1979). "Quantification of the Hierarchy of Tonal Functions within a Diatonic Context." *Journal of Experimental Psychology: Human Perception and Performance* 5:579–94.

Kuhn, Thomas S. (1970). *The Structure of Scientific Revolutions,* 2nd ed. Chicago: University of Chicago Press.

Kuhns, Richard (1978). "Music as a Representational Art." *British Journal of Aesthetics* 18:120–5.

157

Lakatos, Imre, and Alan Musgrave, eds. (1970). *Criticism and the Growth of Knowledge*. Cambridge University Press.

Lerdahl, Fred (1993). "Toward a Theory of Functional Musical Groups." Paper presented at the Society for Music Theory annual meeting, Montreal, November 5.

Lerdahl, Fred, and Ray Jackendoff (1983). *A Generative Theory of Tonal Music*. Cambridge, Mass.: MIT Press.

Levinson, Jerrold (1993). "Edmund Gurney and the Appreciation of Music." *Iyyun* 42:181–205.

Levy, Kenneth (1983). *Music: A Listener's Introduction*. New York: Harper & Row.

Lewis, David (1983a). "Attitudes De Dicto and De Se." In Lewis (1983c), pp. 133–59.

(1983b). "General Semantics." In Lewis (1983c), pp. 189–232.

(1983c). *Philosophical Papers*, Vol. 1. Oxford: Oxford University Press.

Loar, Brian (1981). *Mind and Meaning*. Cambridge University Press.

Locke, John (1975 [1700]). *An Essay Concerning Human Understanding*. Oxford: Oxford University Press.

Marantz, Alec (1985). "'Cognition in Music': Reply to Serafine." *Cognition* 19:73–86.

Marr, David (1982). *Vision*. San Francisco: Freeman.

Meyer, Leonard B. (1956). *Emotion and Meaning in Music*. Chicago: University of Chicago Press.

(1973). *Explaining Music: Essays and Explorations*. Berkeley: University of California Press.

Millikan, Ruth Garrett (1991). "Perceptual Content and Fregean Myth." *Mind* 100:439–59.

Moore, G. E. (1942). "A Reply to My Critics." In *The Philosophy of G. E. Moore*, ed. Paul Arthur Schilpp. La Salle, Ill.: Open Court, pp. 535–677.

Mursell, James L. (1937). *The Psychology of Music*. New York: Norton.

Nagel, Thomas (1974). "What Is It Like to Be a Bat?" *Philosophical Review* 83:435–50.

Narmour, Eugene (1990). *The Analysis and Cognition of Basic Melodic Structures: The Implication-Realization Model*. Chicago: University of Chicago Press.

Neumeyer, David, and Susan Tepping (1992). *A Guide to Schenkerian Analysis*. Englewood Cliffs, N.J.: Prentice-Hall.

Palmer, Stephen E. (1977). "Hierarchical Structure in Perceptual Representation." *Cognitive Psychology* 9:441–74.

Peacocke, Christopher (1983). *Sense and Content*. Oxford: Clarendon Press.

(1986). "Analogue Content." *Proceedings of the Aristotelian Society Supplementary Volume* 60:1–17.

(1989). "Perceptual Content." In Joseph Almog et al., eds., *Themes from Kaplan.* Oxford: Oxford University Press, pp. 297–329.

(1992a). "Scenarios, Concepts, and Perception." In Crane, ed. (1992), pp. 105–35.

(1992b). *A Study of Concepts.* Cambridge, Mass.: MIT Press.

Peel, John, and Wayne Slawson (1984). Review of *A Generative Theory of Tonal Music* by Fred Lerdahl and Ray Jackendoff. *Journal of Music Theory* 28:271–94.

Pitcher, George (1971). *A Theory of Perception.* Princeton, N.J.: Princeton University Press.

Pitson, Anthony (1990). "Perception: Belief and Experience." *Southern Journal of Philosophy* 28:55–76.

Polanyi, Michael (1962). *Personal Knowledge,* corrected ed. Chicago: University of Chicago Press.

Quine, W. V. (1966 [1956]). "Quantifiers and Propositional Attitudes." In *Ways of Paradox.* New York: Random House.

Reti, Rudolph (1951). *The Thematic Process in Music.* New York: Macmillan.

Rosch, E., et al. (1976). "Basic Objects in Natural Categories." *Cognitive Psychology* 8:382–439.

Ryle, Gilbert (1949). *The Concept of Mind.* New York: Barnes & Noble.

Salmon, Nathan (1986). *Frege's Puzzle.* Cambridge, Mass.: MIT Press.

Salzer, Felix (1962). *Structural Hearing: Tonal Coherence in Music,* corrected ed., 2 vols. New York: Dover.

Schenker, Heinrich (1979 [1935]). *Free Composition [Der freie Satz],* 2 vols. Trans. and ed. Ernst Oster. New York: Longman.

Schiffer, Stephen (1992). "Belief Ascription." *Journal of Philosophy* 89:499–521.

Schrade, Leo, ed. (1956). *Polyphonic Music of the Fourteenth Century.* Vol. 3: *The Works of Guillaume de Machaut.* Monaco: L'oiseau-Lyre.

Schulenberg, David (1986). "Modes, Prolongations, and Analysis." *Journal of Musicology* 4:303–29.

Searle, John (1984). *Minds, Brains, and Science.* Cambridge, Mass.: Harvard University Press.

Shapere, Dudley (1966). "Meaning and Scientific Change." In R. Colodny, ed., *Mind and Cosmos: Essays in Contemporary Science and Philosophy.* Pittsburgh: University of Pittsburgh Press, pp. 41–85.

Sloboda, John A. (1985). *The Musical Mind: The Cognitive Psychology of Music.* Oxford: Clarendon Press.

Smith, Michael A. (1986). "Peacocke on Red and Red'." *Synthese* 68:559–76.

Soames, Scott (1984). "Linguistics and Psychology," *Linguistics and Philosophy* 7:155–79.

Stalnaker, Robert (1984). *Inquiry.* Cambridge, Mass.: MIT Press.

Stich, Stephen P. (1971). "What Every Speaker Knows." *Philosophical Review* 80:476–96.

——— (1978). "Beliefs and Subdoxastic States." *Philosophy of Science* 45:499–518.

Strawson, P. F. (1959). *Individuals.* London: Routledge.

Swartz, Robert J., ed. (1965). *Perceiving, Sensing, and Knowing.* Garden City, N.Y.: Doubleday.

Tanner, Michael (1985). "Understanding Music." *Proceedings of the Aristotelian Society Supplementary Volume* 59:216–32.

Tighe, Thomas J., and W. Jay Dowling, eds. (1993). *Psychology and Music: The Understanding of Melody and Rhythm.* Hillsdale, N.J.: Erlbaum.

von Ehrenfels, Christian (1937). "On Gestalt-Qualities," trans. M. Focht. *Psychological Review* 44:521–4. Originally published as "Über Gestaltqualitäten." *Vierteljahrschrift für Wissenschaftliche Philosophie* 14 (1890):249–92.

Walton, Kendall (1970). "Categories of Art." *Philosophical Review* 79:334–67.

——— (1988). "The Presentation and Portrayal of Sound Patterns." In Jonathan Dancy et al., eds., *Human Agency: Language, Duty, and Value.* Stanford, Calif.: Stanford Universtiy Press, pp. 237–57.

——— (1993). "Understanding Humour and Understanding Music." In Michael Krausz, ed., *The Interpretation of Music: Philosophical Essays.* Oxford: Clarendon Press, pp. 259–69.

Weiskrantz, Lawrence (1988). "Neuropsychology of Vision and Memory." In A. J. Marcel and E. Bisiach, eds., *Consciousness in Contemporary Science.* Oxford: Oxford University Press, pp. 183–99.

Wertheimer, Max (1938 [1925]). "Gestalt Theory." In Willis D. Ellis, ed., *A Source Book of Gestalt Psychology.* New York: Harcourt, Brace, pp. 1–11. Originally published as "Über Gestalttheorie." *Symposion* 1(1925):39–60.

Winston, Patrick H. (1975). "Learning Structural Descriptions from Examples." In P. H. Winston, ed., *The Psychology of Computer Vision.* New York: McGraw-Hill, pp. 157–209.

Winter, Robert (1992). *Music for Our Time.* Belmont, Calif.: Wadsworth.

Wittgenstein, Ludwig (1958). *Philosophical Investigations,* 3rd ed., trans. and ed. G. E. M. Anscombe. New York: Macmillan.

Zeki, Semir (1993). *A Vision of the Brain.* Oxford: Blackwell Scientific.

Index

161